Canada

Mt. Katahdin

Bigelow
Mountain

Monson

Vermont

Mt. Washington

Old Speck
Mountain

Maine

Stratton
Mountain

Hanover

Pennsylvania

New York

New
Hampshire

Harmon
Hill

Mt.
Greylock

Massachusetts

Delaware
Water Gap

Mt. Everett

Center Point
Knob

Bear Mountain
State Park

Harpers
Ferry

Wind
Gap

High Point
State Park

Gathland
State Park

Connecticut

Rhode
Island

nandoah
onal Park

Maryland

New Jersey

Delaware

North

Appalachian Trail
the
Calling Me Back To The Hills

the Appalachian Trail

Calling Me Back To The Hills

TEXT AND POETRY BY
Earl Shaffer

PHOTOGRAPHY BY
Bart Smith

WWW.WESTCLIFFEPUBLISHERS.COM

CONTENTS

FOREWORD..........8

PREFACE..........10

INTRODUCTION..........12

CALLING ME BACK TO THE HILLS

Springer Mountain, Georgia, to Fontana Dam, North Carolina......19

Fontana Dam, North Carolina, to Damascus, Virginia......35

Damascus, Virginia, to Pearisburg, Virginia..........51

Pearisburg, Virginia, to Rockfish Gap, Virginia..........59

Rockfish Gap, Virginia, to the Maryland/Pennsylvania border......67

Maryland/Pennsylvania border to the Delaware River..............75

Delaware River to the New York/Connecticut border.............83

New York/Connecticut border to the Massachusetts/Vermont border...91

Massachusetts/Vermont border to the Connecticut River..........99

Connecticut River to the New Hampshire/Maine border.............107

New Hampshire/Maine border to Mount Katahdin................115

AFTERWORD BY LINDA ELLERBEE..........124

THE APPALACHIAN TRAIL CONFERENCE..........126

ACKNOWLEDGMENTS..........128

Opposite: *The Appalachian Trail on Hall Mountain in Maine*
First Frontispiece: *View east from Wesser Bald Lookout, North Carolina*
Second Frontispiece: *Mount Katahdin and the Penobscot River in Maine*
Third Frontispiece: *Catawba rhododendron brighten the Roan Mountain
highlands in Tennessee*

FOREWORD

The Appalachian Trail, called simply "the A.T." by those who hike on it today, is an American cultural icon—a unique wilderness corridor set aside for foot travel only, stretching 2,160 unbroken miles along the ridgeline of the Appalachian mountain chain from Springer Mountain in Georgia to Mount Katahdin in Maine. Since its inception in 1921, the A.T. has drawn millions of adventurers from around the world to walk its magical miles, and they are never disappointed by its enchantments. It takes them on a journey of discovery through a diversity of natural landscapes—crossing lofty mountain peaks and passing through verdant river valleys as it links together some of this nation's finest Eastern wilderness environments—and it introduces these pilgrims to the simple way of life that is still characteristic of rural America off the beaten track. Most of all, it offers them a refuge from manmade clutter—a chance to look inward and take stock of themselves removed from the constant change and confusion of their workaday world and, more often than not, to rediscover themselves amidst the harmonies and simple certainties of nature and its timeless ways.

Earl Shaffer, like many since, was drawn to the Appalachian Trail because he needed to rediscover himself. Born in 1918, he grew up in rural Pennsylvania, where he spent the days of his formative years living an almost idyllic life in harmony with all that surrounded him. As a young lad, the woods and fields were his playground and nature

◆◆◆

Trillium and bluets on Yellow Mountain, North Carolina

◆◆◆

was his friend. Then, as a young man, his country called him to military service in the South Pacific during World War II. Earl served with distinction as a radar technician, but his world was turned upside down by years of wartime combat experience. Earl returned from the war with advanced technological training and expanded horizons, but empty of spirit. As he tried to adjust to the emerging complexity that was the hallmark of postwar America, he found himself increasingly in conflict with this phenomenon and began to yearn for the simpler life and values that had given him sustenance during his early years. It was probably during this period that Earl first sensed that America's mindless rush to modernization, often at the expense of its wild lands and wilderness heritage, was perhaps a journey he did not wish to take. Faced with these inner contradictions, Earl inevitably looked once again to the woods and mountains for answers, as he had always done in his youth.

During the winter of 1947, a magazine article focused Earl's attention on the challenge of hiking the entire Appalachian Trail in one journey, and he immediately responded to the call. He sensed that the A.T. would, by its scope, satisfy the need for grand adventure that the war had awakened in him, and, by its remoteness, give him solace and the time for extended reflection that he needed to sort out his place and purpose in the scheme of things. So, the following spring he shouldered his pack and headed for Georgia to begin his attempt to follow the route of the A.T. to its northern end. His journey was intended as a personal quest. Little did Earl realize that he would be making history as he hiked the white-blazed footpath day after day —over mountains, across streams, into towns and villages, through rain or shine, all the way to Maine—but that is what he did. When he reached the summit of Mount Katahdin and touched the terminus sign on August 5, 1948, he became the first person to have hiked the entire Appalachian Trail in one continuous journey.

Earl's status in life would be forever changed by his achievement, which in the annals of hiking holds the same place of importance that Charles Lindbergh's first transatlantic flight enjoys in the world of aviation. Earl Shaffer's name has become synonymous with adventure, courage, bravery, perseverance, strength of character, and all of the other traits we expect in our heroes—and, for more than a half-century, he has worn the mantle of fame for being "the first" with dignity and humility. Perhaps even more telling about the man himself, he has remained true to his upbringing and wilderness convictions, eschewing the pursuits of worldly fame— prominence, riches, adulation— and choosing instead to live a private life of simplicity and closeness to nature. On a personal level Earl is a shy man, with little need for public attention, and his inclination to chart his own course and live alone has led many to think of him as somewhat of an eccentric recluse, but nothing could be further from the truth. His love of life is revealed by his many talents—hiking and backpacking, environmental activism, composing music, writing poetry—and by the ever-present twinkle in his eyes as he talks about his beloved mountains and woods.

In the spring of 1998, Earl Shaffer once again heeded the call to come back to the hills. Fifty years after he had set forth on his historic first Appalachian Trail hike as a young man, he hiked its entire length again, this time to say one last good-bye to the wilderness footpath with which his life had become so closely intertwined. He discovered that the Appalachian Trail, like himself, had aged gracefully, though he found the Trail more challenging than it was in his younger days. He also found that he was not the only person hiking from Georgia to Maine, as had been the case in 1948. Thousands of thru-hikers were following the path he had blazed so many years ago, a tribute to his achievement.

Through the words in this book, Earl recorded his impressions and the events of his farewell hike. In the pages that follow, you, too, will experience Earl's unique anniversary journey and will have the privilege of getting to know a true hiking legend whose life epitomizes the very best of the ideals that define the Appalachian Trail.

—Dan "Wingfoot" Bruce

◆◆◆

The Trail crosses an old stone fence on Baldy Mountain in Massachusetts

◆◆◆

Dan Bruce, author of The Thru-Hiker's Handbook, *is founder of the Center for Appalachian Trail Studies, a clearinghouse of information about the Appalachian Trail. Please visit the website at www.trailplace.com or write to Center for Appalachian Trail Studies, P.O. Box 525, Hot Springs, NC 28743.*

PREFACE

The cover story for the December 1998 issue of *Outside* magazine read, "Wish List: 100 Ideas Toward a Bigger Life." Before I turned the pages I guessed that walking the Appalachian Trail would make the top ten. Indeed, doing a thru-hike came in at number eight, just behind "Touching the Amazon River" and "Retracing Powell's Western Geographic Expedition." At the top of the recommended list of trails was the Appalachian Trail—which is appropriate, as it is and will remain the "Granddaddy of all Trails."

Historically, the number of people attempting to thru-hike the A.T. during a given year has fluctuated over several-year cycles. In the past few years, though, the number of hikers has increased dramatically, with no sign of letting up. Although the upsurge in popularity has many reasons, two motivating factors bandied about are the popularity of Bill Bryson's book *A Walk in the Woods* and the media coverage surrounding Earl Shaffer's historic 50th-anniversary hike along the A.T. in 1998.

Before I began my Appalachian adventure I had never heard of Earl Shaffer. In fact, I knew very little about the Appalachian Trail. Having lived most of my life among the Douglas fir and saw-toothed peaks of the Cascade Range in Washington state, my only association with the Appalachian Mountains was a love of bluegrass music. While hiking and photographing for *Along the Pacific Crest Trail*, a coffee-table book, I encountered many thru-hikers who had recently completed the A.T.

The Russell boots worn by Earl Shaffer on his 1948 thru-hike

Their experiences had whetted their appetites for exploring more open trails.

Life on the trail has a simplicity about it that can become contagious. I usually could recognize A.T. hikers just by the names they gave when introducing themselves. When I ran into hikers on the Pacific Crest Trail with names like "Rin Tin Tin," "Let it Be," and "Horse Feathers," I knew they had a lot of miles under their pack belts!

The more I heard about the spring flowers of North Carolina, the blue ridges of Virginia, the bears of New Jersey, the autumn colors of New England, and the wildness of Maine, the more I was intrigued. Besides, after hiking and photographing the Pacific Crest Trail, I, too, needed more open trail to lure me on. So, in the spring of 1998, I adopted the trail name "Mountain Paparazzi"—subsequently shortened to "Paparazzi"—and set my sights and lenses on the Appalachian Trail.

There are about as many reasons to walk the Appalachian Trail as there are people walking it. I noticed that some folks on the A.T. had gone through a recent major life change such as retirement, graduation, or divorce, and walking the Trail allowed them time to contemplate their lives. Some people take time off from work and hike the A.T. to escape the traffic, faxes, phones, and general chaos of life. Others are just looking for good old-fashioned adventure. My primary reason for going was photography.

I can't keep a musical beat. I sing only in the car, alone, with the windows rolled up. Drawing stick figures is a challenge. And I had a dickens of a time writing this Preface. But I have a crazy desire to express my awe and wonder at being alive on this great earth. That's why I love photography and hiking. So when people tell me I'm a glutton for punishment because of the 65 pounds of gear I carry on my back, I say to myself, "Don't worry—knee replacement surgery is becoming affordable, and I'm a happy man—most of the time."

The Appalachian Trail has an aura, a mystique about it. From the outset my goal was to capture some of that on film. I knew it would be a challenge, as still photography works only in the visual dimension. I couldn't capture the feel of an autumn breeze, the smell of a deciduous forest, or the taste of ice-cold spring water. But I knew that the visual appeal would be impressive along the 2,160-plus miles of the A.T.

My modus operandi was to hike 200- to 300-mile sections, photographing along the way and scouting locations for dramatic photographs at different times of day or during different seasons. I then would hitchhike or shuttle back to my car and later day-hike to locations I wanted to rephotograph. I revisited many sections throughout the year to photograph the A.T. in all its seasonal variations. I completed the entire A.T. in a year and a half, although the actual hiking time was six months. I used a Nikon F3 camera because it's fairly

McAfee Knob in Washington-Jefferson National Forest

♦♦♦

rugged and the battery weight is minimal. The lenses I employed were a 24mm, a 35–70mm zoom, and an 80–200mm zoom with 1.4 extender, plus a 400mm for a few day hikes. The tripod was a Gitzo 328 and the film was Fuji Velvia.

I had the very good fortune of meeting Earl Shaffer twice on his Anniversary Trip, and when I learned that he would pen the words in this book, I was thrilled. The first place I met Earl was Webster Cliffs, an especially brutal section of the Trail in the rugged White Mountains. When I saw Earl's pith helmet coming up the cliffs, I realized that I was finally going to meet this man I'd heard so much about. We shook hands and he asked me where I was from, which led to a conversation about the Pacific Crest Trail (he had hiked the trail through northern Washington with his nephew). Earl's demeanor was such that I almost forgot I was talking to a Trail legend. After bidding farewell, as I watched Earl head up the cliffs, I pinched myself.

Leaders are of many types. Some lead by decree and some lead by example. Earl is one of the latter. When he began walking the A.T. in 1948, no one had hiked the entire Trail in one year and many people believed it couldn't be done. Earl quietly walked into the history books by completing the Trail in just four months. Thousands of people have since followed in his footsteps. Fifty years later at the ripe young age of 79, Earl again walked into the history books as the oldest person known to have completed the Trail in one year. During a special ceremony in 1999, he presented his boots and backpack from 1948 to the Smithsonian Institution in Washington, D.C. To collaborate with someone of such historical distinction as Earl is an honor and a privilege, and a bit daunting.

The photographs in this book are arranged in a south-to-north sequence that corresponds to Earl's 1998 thru-hike. My photographs accompany Earl's account of his Anniversary Trip and his original poems—a fitting tribute to the Trail. Our hope is that Earl's words and my photographs will evoke the mystery and majesty that is the Appalachian Trail.

—Bart "Paparazzi" Smith

Visit Bart Smith's website at www.bartsmithphotography.com.

INTRODUCTION
Pioneer: 79 and Climbing

by Michael Vitez, Staff writer, *The Philadelphia Inquirer*

ALONG THE APPALACHIAN TRAIL—Earl Shaffer reached the Bearfence shelter about 2 p.m. He peeled off his 40-pound pack and gobbled four hard-boiled eggs and a package of 20 crackers, spooning jelly on each one or directly into his mouth. He unrolled his bedroll on the wooden floor and slept for three hours with his boots on.

Shaffer had hiked 860 miles in the previous 68 days, over the highest mountains in the southeastern United States. He wore out his first pair of boots about 200 miles back.

This folk hero and reclusive Pennsylvanian, now 79, was the first man ever to hike the Appalachian Trail continuously from Georgia to Maine, covering the historic mountain footpath in four months and four hours in the spring and summer of 1948.

Fifty years later, to commemorate this event, Shaffer is backpacking once again the 2,160 miles from Springer Mountain, Georgia, to Katahdin, Maine.

"I just like to walk in the woods and sleep on mountaintops," he explained.

To many hikers, lean, leather-necked Earl Shaffer—just five months shy of his 80th birthday—is a legend.

"When the trail was completed in 1937, for years it was thought impossible that anyone could do it from end to end," said Dan Bruce, author of *The Thru-Hiker's Handbook*. "Earl expanded the possibilities for the average person. He's the Charles Lindbergh of American hiking."

More than 1,500 hikers a year now attempt a thru-hike, though experts say only one in 10 succeeds. Most are strong young men and women, many of whom have heard of Shaffer and are proud to shake his hand or share a shelter with him.

Andrew Long, from Clayton, New Jersey, scribbled this in the Bearfence shelter logbook:

"Without getting too dramatic, quite simply, it is a pleasure to meet and observe Mr. Shaffer."

After waking up from his nap Wednesday afternoon, Shaffer talked about the trail and his life. He hiked it a second time in 1965, that time north to south, in just 99 days.

"The trail does a lot of good," he explained. "It's scenic. It helps preserve the pioneer spirit. It commemorates the old trails of the West. Those old trails brought civilization through the wilderness. This trail is wilderness through civilization."

After talking a while, he ate two more hard-boiled eggs and more crackers with peanut butter, slugged down a quart of water, and slept 12 hours, this time with his boots off.

At 7 a.m. Thursday Shaffer woke, poured baby powder into his boots (he never wears socks), and packed his bedroll. Most days he breakfasts on oatmeal soaked overnight in water. But on this morning he munched on more crackers and peanut butter, put on his trademark pith helmet, and set out north.

◆ ◆ ◆

Earl Shaffer at the Birch Run Shelter in Pennsylvania

◆ ◆ ◆

Less than a mile up the trail he unbuttoned his blue flannel shirt—the same faded shirt he had worn since he started May 2. He wiped his brow and broke off a small branch of leaves to fan himself as he walked.

"Oh, boy."

On level ground, he flies along. Up the mountains, he plods, often stopping at switchbacks to catch his wind.

Heading up Hazeltop Mountain on Thursday morning, the third-highest peak in Shenandoah National Park in Virginia, he stopped and took a long breath.

"I don't like uphills very good," he said.

For hours and sometimes days, Shaffer will hike alone, without seeing anyone, hearing only his own breathing, his feet hitting the dirt, the wind in the trees. He will stop to admire the trees uprooted in ice storms, a deer track or wildflower, or an eagle flying overhead.

Shaffer has been alone most of his life. Never married, he has no one waiting for him, counting on him, putting expectations on him. He loves solitude, both on the trail and at his rustic home in York Springs in Adams County, about 15 miles north of Gettysburg and a few miles from the Appalachian Trail. He lives on a small farm with a cat and a goat.

Until two years ago, he lived without electricity. "Now his bill is about $7 a month," said his brother John Shaffer of York. "He doesn't even have a refrigerator. He doesn't

have anything that needs refrigeration."

Four years ago, Earl Shaffer finally agreed to keep a telephone—a cellular phone his brother gave him. When he started this golden anniversary hike, Earl carried the cellphone at his brother's insistence. The phone arrived in the mail at John's house a week later.

"Too heavy to carry," Earl explained.

His pack is much lighter than many others' on the trail. He carries no stove, and only one change of clothes. In addition to cold food and his bedroll, he carries one pot, two light tarps, a trail guide, baby powder, a knife, and a foam pad from an old chair.

He has no tent. He prefers to lay his bedroll on a mountaintop. If it rains, he covers himself with a tarp.

"The cowboys did it, didn't they?"

Earl rests at the halfway point of the A.T., Center Point Knob, Pennsylvania, 1948

Near the end of his historic 1948 thru-hike, Earl Shaffer registers at Baxter State Park, Maine

Form No. 10-369

UNITED STATES
DEPARTMENT OF THE INTERIOR
NATIONAL PARK SERVICE
N⁰ 979
SHENANDOAH NATIONAL PARK

CAMPING PERMIT

Name _Earl Shaffer_
Address _R.D. #1 York, Pa_ and others
Period _5-15-48_, 19___, to _10-15-48_ 19___
Location _Along AT_

THIS PERMIT VOID DURING FIRE SEASON AND NOT GOOD IN RESTRICTED AREAS

In accepting this free camping permit, permittee agrees to abide by the park regulations which are briefed on reverse hereof.

Issued by _Peter F. Johnson_ Title _Ranger_

This permit may be revoked by order of the Superintendent when, in his judgment, the fire hazard makes such action necessary.

(SEE OVER)

6—9531

Hiker, 29, Who Completed 2,000 Miles Of Appalachian Trail Thinks Maine 'Swell'

By MRS. DEAN CHASE
(NEWS Correspondent)

MILLINOCKET, Aug. 5.—Earl Shaffer climbed mile-high Mt. Katahdin this after a 2,000-mile hike over the Appalachian Tr to be the first

Hiker to Speak

arl V. Shaffer, of York, covered the Appalachian from Georgia

LONG DISTANCE HIKER— Earl Shaffer, 29, son of Daniel Shaffer, York RD 1, who has solved the problem of killing those leisure hours by taking a long walk—from Georgia to Maine. The husky young army veteran from Mt. Oglethorpe, Ga., expects to reach

When he suspects rain, as he did (correctly) last Wednesday night, he tries to sleep in a shelter along the trail.

The heaviest thing he carries is two quarts of water. He likes to drink a gallon of water a day, refilling his jugs along the trail.

Shaffer avoids public showers at campgrounds because he is afraid of athlete's foot—a sure way to end his trip. Instead he carries a washcloth and makes do.

"Find a stream, try to stay halfway civilized."

In the back pocket of his blue work pants he carries a small notebook in which he chronicles his trip. Shaffer is a poet who has written more than 1,000 poems, most of which are in a file cabinet at his brother's home. He wrote and published a book about his first trip, including his photographs, titled *Walking With Spring*.

Shaffer took his first trip to pull himself out of a post–World War II depression. He spent three years in the Pacific, in the most difficult conditions, building airstrips and radar stations. He covered 60,000 miles by sea and air, often with little food, battling tropical illnesses.

From
Benton MacKaye,
℅ Kenneth W. Ross,
56 Mackey Ave.,
Port Washington, N.Y.

PORT WASHINGTON N.Y.
JAN 29
630PM
1954

UNITED STATES POSTAGE
THREE 3 CENTS

Mr. Earl Shaffer,
York, Penna.

His best friend from York, his soul-mate since age five, was killed on the beach at Iwo Jima.

"When the war was over, I couldn't settle down or do anything," Shaffer said. "I told myself I've got to do something. Why not do something that's never been done?...It straightened me out, more or less."

The trail—which today runs through mostly public land—was conceived in 1921 by Benton MacKaye, a forester and regional planner, and has always been maintained by thousands of volunteers who belong to 31 clubs, their efforts coordinated by the Appalachian Trail Conference in Harpers Ferry, West Virginia.

After World War II, the trail was a shambles, many sections neglected or abandoned. Few Americans knew it existed.

On the day Shaffer set out 50 years ago, he passed a man in Georgia picnicking with his family.

"Howdy," the man said. "Where you headin'?"

"Maine," Shaffer responded.

Eyes popped out. The man stuttered. Neither he nor his wife realized there was such a trail that went to Maine or that they were on it.

"You mean to tell me," said the wife, "you're a-walkin' all the way to the state of Maine, all by yourself, over them mountains, carrying that thing?"

"Yes, ma'am."

"I'se glad I got sense," the woman told him.

Ever since then, Shaffer has been known on the trail as Crazy One.

In 1948, Shaffer hiked the trail much more swiftly. One reason is because the trail is more difficult today. Volunteers have relocated many stretches to more scenic, more rugged patches of mountain.

Shaffer is also a half-century older.

"About a week ago I began to have an ache in my left lung which gradually moved," he wrote in his journal recently. "I began to breathe easier and deeper. For years my lung capacity had lessened and it was attributed to advancing age. Apparently my lung was in a state of

Opposite: *One of Earl Shaffer's ongoing personal communications with Benton MacKaye, founder of the A.T.*

Half-century later, this stoic pioneer is back on the Trail

TRAIL from F1

To many hikers, lean, leather-necked Earl Shaffer — just five months shy of his 80th birthday — is a legend.

"When the trail was completed in 1937, for years it was thought impossible that anyone could do it from end to end," said Dan Bruce, author of *The Thru-Hiker's Handbook.* "Earl expanded the possibilities f the average person. He's t Lindbergh of American h

More than 1,500 hikers a attempt a thru-hike, thoug say only one in 10 su

The Appalachian Trail

Hopes to finish in early October, Mount Katahdin

MAINE
Augusta

CANADA   VT.

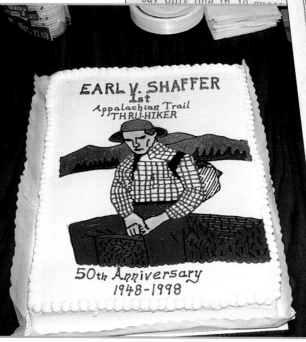

This cake was one of many tributes that Earl Shaffer received as he hiked along the Appalachian Trail.

APPALACHIAN TRAIL
DAMASCUS
VA

Honoring Earl Shaffer

'48/'98
GA - ME

Thirteenth Annual Appalachian Trail Days Celebration

Damascus, Virginia
May 7 - 16, 1999

"The Friendliest Town On The Trail"

The 1999 Trail Days Celebration is Dedicated to Earl Shaffer - first person to thru-hike the Appalachian Trail.

PARKING:
Wilson Street - Daily
McBee (US 58) Saturday - 15th
(access to Creeper Trail)
dy Avenue (daily)

collapse and now is functioning again, a miracle. I feel rejuvenated and encouraged to keep hiking. The human body is indeed a wonderful thing."

He had hoped to reach Katahdin in Maine by early September, but he's a bit behind schedule. Now he'd be happy with early October. He is expected to reach Pennsylvania by early next week.

After hiking eight miles Thursday morning, Shaffer, hot and sweaty in the humid Virginia heat, stopped and looked back.

"Only about twelve hundred to go!"

He laughed slyly and kept walking.

Reprinted with permission from The Philadelphia Inquirer, *July 14, 1998.*

During Earl Shaffer's Anniversary Trip, many journalists met and interviewed him on the Trail. One of them was Michael Vitez of The Philadelphia Inquirer, *who won a Pulitzer Prize in 1997 for his coverage of aging issues. This article was first published more than three months before Earl reached Mount Katahdin in Maine.*

Earl crossing Katahdin Stream in Baxter State Park, Maine, in 1948

Earl Shaffer on the Appalachian Trail in Maine, 1998, a half-century after his historic thru-hike of 1948

Calling Me Back to the Hills

The whip-poor-will's call and the laughing owl's song
are calling me back to the hills,
To the best place of all where I know I belong,
where the water falls, tumbles, and spills.

In my innermost dreams is the sigh of the pines
as the soft siren song of the trails,
With the murmuring streams where the laurel entwines
far out in the wilderness vales.

In the banner that furls at the closing of day,
returning at break of the dawn,
In the woodsmoke that curls to the sky and away
is the penchant that's luring me on.

Through the mist of the morning that creepingly swirls
Like wraiths through each little ravine
O'er the meadows unshorn where the dewdrops are pearls,
I'll gaze on a half-hidden scene.

I'll awake to the song of the thrush in the tree,
exultant at daylight's return,
And the bond will be strong when he's singing for me
that paean for which ever I yearn.

Then I'll seek out that most perfect valley of all
that I've pictured so long in my mind,
And submit to the mystic yet relevant call
Whose lure is to seek and to find.

I never shall mind if the terrain be strange,
my compass is trusty and true;
I'll just travel blind and scout out the range
and trust to my luck to come through.

I'll sit by my campfire each nomadic night
and muse of the present and past,
And follow the spire of that soul-stirring light
'til I reach that one valley at last.

Springer Mountain, Georgia
to Fontana Dam, North Carolina

On May 2, 1998, two carloads of relatives escorted me to Springer Mountain, Georgia. I was about to retrace my path of long ago, from the southern terminus of the Appalachian Trail in Georgia to the northern terminus at Mount Katahdin, Maine, more than 2,000 miles away.

Connecting the southern and northern points is a mountain footpath that soars higher than 6,000 feet and dips almost to sea level. The terrain varies from subtropical rain forest in the South to the timberline peaks of the North.

This is a nature trail. Plant life ranges from the giant trees of the South to the tiny tundra-type plants seen among the timberline rocks. Wildlife covers the spectrum from mosquitoes to moose, hummingbirds to eagles. Footing can be anything from boulders to bogs to streams. The weather is just as variable. The ultimate challenge is to travel the Trail's entire length in a continuous journey, carrying a pack.

I was almost 80 years old when I set out on the Trail in 1998, 50 years since my "Long Cruise," the first end-to-end trek over the famous Appalachian Trail. Why did I go again? I couldn't stay home. I couldn't pass up the chance to celebrate this anniversary on the Trail itself—or at least try to.

◆◆◆

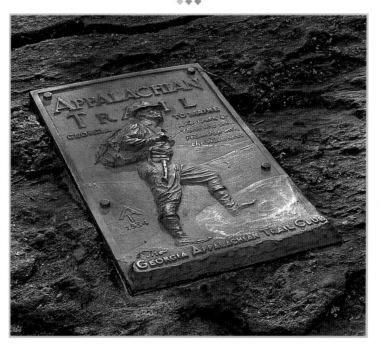

The southern terminus of the Trail, Springer Mountain, Georgia

◆◆◆

The odds were long. Only a few hundred of the thousands who start off each year succeed. Never say you *will* do it. You can only try.

With me for the first few days was my nephew, Bob, who once hiked with me for a week when he was 16. Since then, he has become an expert outdoorsman, with experience including mountain search-and-rescue and ski patrol. After hours of picture-taking and talk, we finally got under way in mid-afternoon and hiked only a few miles before stopping at a campsite. We bedded in the woods like white-tailed deer.

I carried no tent, just a pair of tarps. My pack was a mountain troop rucksack from World War II, stripped of all but the stuff sack, frame, and harness. I've used this type of pack on all my trips because it handles best in rough terrain. It carries low, with weight on the hips for best balance, it has no zippers to jam, and the frame keeps the pack away from your back. In it were 50 pounds of food and gear—but not for long. You travel light on a long trek, and quickly decide what is essential.

That first night on the Trail was damp and chilly, and as we started at sunrise, a misty rain was falling. The Trail goes over and around the Georgia mountains, high and jumbled, a regular maze—you seem to get nowhere. You look yonder through the haze and say, "That isn't a cloud, it's a

Woods beside access trail to the start of the Appalachian Trail, Amicalola State Park, Georgia

mountain." One man from the Ozarks said he was intimidated and almost headed home.

Flowers were in bloom on the eastern slopes and the trees were beginning to bud—the time of year when the earth comes alive. That first full day, we covered about 15 miles and stopped beyond Woody Gap.

An early start the next morning took us over Blood Mountain, at 4,461 feet the highest point on the Trail in Georgia. It is the sacred peak of the Cherokee Indians, who lived in the Southern mountains until the U.S. Army drove them west after gold was discovered in the area. The Cherokees fought a desperate battle against the Creeks on Blood Mountain hundreds of years ago.

> "*The odds were long. Only a few hundred of the thousands who start off each year succeed. Never say you will do it. You can only try.*"

About halfway down to Neels Gap, the Trail passes Balance Rock, a gigantic boulder that looks as though a gentle push would topple it. According to Cherokee myth, Neels Gap was the meeting place of the Ancient Animal Council, led by the Great Frog. Near Balance Rock, Gail Johnson, a friend of relatives in South Carolina and a thru-hiker whose trail name is "Gutsy," brought us food supplies including an applesauce cake from my niece, Debbie.

Ascending from Neels Gap, I recalled meeting Gene Espy there in 1965 on my north-to-south thru-hike, the "Autumn Stroll." Gene was the second person to hike the completed Trail end-to-end, in 1951, and he had brought his daughter to see the Trail. The meeting was fortunate: My clothes were in tatters and my food was almost gone. Gene drove me down to a store and back, a critical boost for trail-weary me. We still correspond and see each other from time to time.

The top of Amicalola Falls in Amicalola State Park, Georgia

Wild geranium in Chattahoochee National Forest

By the roadside at Neels Gap is Walasi-Yi Center, completed in 1937 as an inn and restaurant for the few brave souls who would venture that far on the Trail. At the trail outfitters' store, where hikers often reorganize their gear, send unnecessary gear home, and purchase supplies, the staff asked me to autograph items including a T-shirt with a picture of me on it. Because Walasi-Yi Center is at one of the first major road crossings encountered on the Trail, it is also where many hikers drop out. Bob left for an airport to fly home to Seattle and his job.

I was now hiking alone.

On Levelland Mountain the weather turned ugly. A mean-looking storm seemed headed directly at me but suddenly veered through a nearby gap. My bed that night was damp and chilled by a strong wind.

A daybreak start took me through Raven Cliff Wilderness, where turkey vultures were circling above the trees. Then a lone raven came circling by, its head cocked to look down at the earthbound clod.

At the next road crossing I met my first "trail angel," helpful folks sometimes met along the Trail. A van was parked there and "Even Steven" Korb gave me snacks and trail information.

I followed a long ridgecrest to Low Gap Shelter and 7 miles beyond on easy trail, some of it following an overgrown fire road. Hope it's never needed. My bed that night was by the road on a pad of gathered leaves.

Wistful Mood in May

A tilted half-moon skims the trees,
A mockingbird is trilling far
Among the midnight phantasies
That drift upon a shadow breeze
While I am wondering where you are.

Sunset from Tray Mountain, Georgia

The first road across the Georgia Blue Ridge was built by settlers and Indians at Unicoi Gap. The Trail leads on through Indian Grave Gap to Tray Mountain. On Tray Mountain, the Trail cuts a tunnel through groves of tree-sized rhododendron bushes—20 to 30 feet high and 5 to 6 inches thick—that must be hundreds of years old.

The Tray Mountain Shelter beyond the summit was crowded, so I slept in the woods nearby. In 1948 the shelter here was an old log lean-to—tumbledown and wrecked by cattle, which were permitted to graze on national forest lands. No longer do you hear the tinkle or clang of cow bells, or see hogs rooting for acorns, or have to circle bellering bulls. Light rain was falling in the morning but eased as I started on. My stay at Deep Gap Shelter was wintry.

A truck was parked at Dicks Creek Gap, and Mr. Nickols, who lives near Standing Indian Mountain, offered me a ride into Hiawassee, Georgia, to a supermarket. There, I bought raisins, dark brown sugar, whole-wheat bread, peanut butter, dried soup, and lettuce. Because I had no stove, I carried mostly cold foods. My eating was ration-style, and my only cooking an occasional dozen hard-boiled eggs. On the way back, a violent storm, with hail, roared through the gap. I was lucky to be in Mr. Nickols's truck.

At twilight I arrived at Plumorchard Gap Shelter. It was crowded, so I headed into the woods for another piney bed. Another storm blew in late at night, and in the morning I was soaked. After the sun broke through, I stopped to dry out.

This trip was certainly different from 50 years ago, when I had the Trail to myself and could build a fire to dry out. Dead wood is scarce now, especially near shelters, which sometimes don't even have

◆ ◆ ◆

Spring oak leaves on Blood Mountain, Georgia

◆ ◆ ◆

firepits. Fires are discouraged, even forbidden in some places. In '48 I would set up a half-circle tepee with my poncho and keep a fire going in front. This is not practical now. I should have brought a tent—lightweight models with folding frames are now available.

The Trail crosses into North Carolina at Bly Gap. There, a gnarled and twisted old oak tree is said to be the most photographed object along the entire Trail. Beyond is a twisty, turny trail up a steep slope to a pinnacle view and groves of rhododendron, not yet in bloom when I was there.

A giant dead chestnut stands at trailside, one of the few remaining of many thousands that towered over the living forest in '48. The chestnut was considered the most valuable tree in the area before a blight from the Orient destroyed the species. Its wood was used for everything from fence rails to fine furniture, and its chestnuts provided food for wildlife as well as for people.

The summit of Standing Indian Mountain —"the grandstand of the southern Appalachians" at more than a mile high— was shrouded by fog. The curve of the ridge beyond encircles the watershed valley of the Nantahala River. "Nantahala" means "land of the noonday sun," which is literally true because the valleys are so deep and narrow. The only way to get anywhere is to use the ridgetops, away from the thickets of greenbriars.

Voices ahead proved to be from a group of boys, probably from a youth rehabilitation program. They stopped to talk and take pictures. Many hikers were on the Trail without packs, so it must have been a weekend. The packs I did see were bulky and high, with pockets that pull and snag.

For miles the ridge was fairly level, so I practically flew, making up time lost in the Georgia maze. A sign on a tree announced,

Tree branch patterns on Tray Mountain, Chattahoochee National Forest, Georgia

Wayah Bald Lookout, North Carolina

"Bear refuge." Two long-legged hikers went striding by, so I stepped aside.

Then came a notoriously rocky, short, steep, and twisty climb to the top of Albert Mountain and a view from the ancient fire tower on the top. Most of the fire towers that once were spaced along the Trail are gone and the few that remain are not manned. Fire spotting is now done by satellite.

On hard climbs I go into "stutter gear": stop and go, stop and go, a pause now and then for a heartbeat or two, take a deep breath— but never stop for long. I lost the trail at a tricky switchback. When in doubt, look about, backtrack, don't hurry.

The sun was setting as I arrived at Big Spring Shelter, so I stopped and slept in the woods nearby. I seldom sleep in a shelter in dry weather because they have board floors. A leaf-padded bed in the woods is much more comfortable. A friend of long ago, newspaperman David S. Fry, once said, "Sleep on the ground; it will energize you. Shelter floors don't." Some hikers carry a pad, which adds weight and bulk to the pack. Actually, a small pad for under the hips—where the misery is worst—is a big help.

At Winding Stair Gap a truck stopped to disembark four hikers. The driver, Paul, drove me down to Franklin, North Carolina, to a store and back. Farther north, a sign described the wide valley eastward as a forest laboratory for the preservation and improvement of watersheds. Surely Benton MacKaye, the father of the Trail, must have been involved here—his kind of conservation project.

Siler Bald gives fine views of the Nantahala watershed. After dipping through Wayah Gap, the Trail switchbacks to the open summit of Wayah Bald, with its stone memorial to a longtime forestry official.

Upon my arrival at Tellico Gap, the sun was sinking. The staccato rat-a-tat-tat of a pileated woodpecker and the twitter of a towhee livened the solitude. Azaleas, from white to flame to red, were brilliant as I prepared my bed by a fallen log.

Diversity of Nature

I pity those who've never seen
The bursting bud and foliage green,
That make up nature's brilliant sheen
Of springtime's blushing beauty.

And pity those who never know
The joy of watching grain fields grow,
Who never see the golden flow
Of harvest's ripened beauty.

And those who've never seen the blaze
Of Indian summer's balmy days
When colored foliage makes a maze
Of flaming autumn beauty.

Or never viewed the noble sight
Of snow-draped fields in bright moonlight
Who've never seen the chast'ning white
Of winter's austere beauty.

I pity those who are not blessed
With sight of nature at its best,
Who are not constantly impressed
With all its varied beauty.

Mountain laurel along the Appalchian Trail
near Dicks Creek Gap, Georgia

Azalea and mountain laurel near Locust Grove Gap, North Carolina

Many switchbacks eased the morning ascent of Wesser Bald. The tower, where on my Long Cruise I had stopped and talked with the lookout, is still there but is no longer manned. The view to the northwest shows the Great Smoky Mountains, the dominant range of the Southern mountains, in silhouette against the skyline. Below is the valley of the Nantahala River, where it begins its tumbling plunge through the gorge to the Tennessee Valley.

On the way down from Wesser Bald is a memorial shelter honoring A. Rufus Morgan, the "Flying Parson," a circuit rider to many mountain churches and a longtime Trail worker. At Trail conferences, he always conducted sunrise services. He lived to be almost 100 years old, like Benton MacKaye—two wonderful men.

The community of Wesser, North Carolina, which was a remote mountain village with a few homes and a country store on my first trip, is now the busy takeoff point for rafting trips down the gorge. There, I mailed my cell phone and transistor radio home. They did not function in the high mountains, plus they were too heavy. After almost 150 miles of hiking, my pack weight was down to an average of 35 pounds. Many hikers carry at least 10 pounds more than that.

At Sassafras Gap Shelter, I stopped to talk with hikers and to get water at the spring, then went on to the summit of Cheoah Bald, which tops out at more than 5,000 feet in elevation. I stopped there to sleep near the highest point. The evening was beautiful from that lofty vantage point: the surrounding valleys dark with shadow, and a far-off mountaintop glowing with the last rays of the setting sun. I like to sleep with the sky—as high up as I can—because I like to look at the stars when I fall asleep.

The twittering of towhees woke me to the flaring of a summit sunrise. At Locust Cove Gap I went down to the spring, leaving my pack at the Trail. Walking without the pack was more difficult because I had adjusted my balance like the pack was part of my body. When shedding a pack at the close of day, it's much like the man who wore his boots tight for the pleasure of taking them off.

The view south from Standing Indian Mountain, North Carolina

Pink ladyslipper near Sweetwater Gap, North Carolina

> **"** *I like to sleep with the sky—as high up as I can—because I like to look at the stars when I fall asleep.* **"**

At Stecoah Gap I met and talked with an Australian chap, a small, friendly man who was carrying a heavy pack. He said he was on an extended tour of America, spending it mostly in the outdoors. Strangely, it is often the smallest people who carry the largest packs. Perhaps it is the total weight of the person and the pack that really counts.

My approach to Cable Gap Shelter was a race with the setting sun. My arrival was by flashlight. A whip-poor-will was calling. They are night creatures, never seen in the daytime. My bed, as usual, was near the shelter. One hiker had pitched his tent nearby.

◆◆◆

Trillium on Yellow Mountain, North Carolina

Looking east from "The Courthouse Bench" on Courthouse Bald, North Carolina

Next page: *The Trail heads toward Snowbird Gap in North Carolina*

Sight of the Hills

Always my eyes range upward
Ever in search of hills;
I have no love for prairies wide
For boundless space on every side,
I love the hills where trees abide
And spring-fed sparkling rills.

Ne'er could I be contented
To stay out on the plain,
For I would ever strive to be
Where peaceful hills are close alee,
There one can always turn and see
Their outline once again.

A restlessness and longing
That only has one balm:
To see the verdant slopes that rise
With dip and curve against the skies
'Til one can almost visualize
The hills of David's Psalm.

Ever my eyes are lifting,
How could they otherwise,
For I could never be content
To dwell in any firmament
That had no graceful silhouette
Of hills against the sky.

Fontana Dam, North Carolina *to* Damascus, Virginia

The Trail soon comes to Fontana Dam, a North Carolina valley town where the workers had lived in the '30s while building the Tennessee Valley Authority dam. In '48 the Trail still followed the Yellow Creek Mountains to Tapoco. Now it crosses the dam. The man at the information desk was amazed to learn that the Appalachian Trail had originated with the same individual who drew up the original charts for the TVA, Benton MacKaye, many years before that project began.

The Trail ascends Shuckstack Mountain to the crest of the Smokies. My bed was about halfway up, on the usual leaf pad. In the morning a big black bear on the ridgetop moved slowly away from me as I approached. When they are not at shelters seeking food, the black bears usually are not aggressive.

Birch Spring Shelter is built of stone with a chainlink fence across the front. The people are caged to keep out the bears. All of the shelters in Great Smoky Mountains National Park are now of this type, replacing the log lean-tos that were there on my previous trips.

My visit to Spence Field—formerly an open area of a thousand acres or so, and now mostly overgrown—brought back memories of an April night 50 years ago when I walked the field by moonlight, my footsteps crunching faintly in the tall,

A snail in Great Smoky Mountains National Park

dry grass. This poem came to me there:

> Walking by moonlight on top of Old Smoky,
> Far on the mountain, alone with the sky,
> While up from the deeps of shadowy valleys,
> Wistful and wild comes the whip-poor-will's cry.

At the shelter some young hikers were resting. They looked downhearted and probably wouldn't be on the Trail much longer. They said never a word so I did the same. I got water at the spring and rambled on.

Beyond Spence Field is Thunderhead, which provides a faraway view to the south. At Silers Bald Shelter I once met a bear face-to-face and stared at it until it panicked and ran. Was it Davy Crockett who once said he had "grinned" a bear? Could be!

From Silers Bald, the trail is narrow and twisty to Clingmans Dome, at 6,643 feet in elevation the highest point on the Appalachian Trail. The mountain is named after Thomas Lanier Clingman, a U.S. senator, Civil War brigadier general, and prospector. Many years ago Senator Clingman of Tennessee and Professor Mitchell of North Carolina had a long dispute as to which state had the highest peak. With Mount Mitchell rising about 40 feet higher than Clingmans Dome, the

Opposite: *A deer along the Appalachian Trail on Thunderhead Mountain*

professor won but fell from a cliff; he is now buried on his mountain.

The sun was setting as I arrived at the topside tower on Clingmans Dome, so that was where I laid my bed.* Always did want to sleep "On Top of Old Smoky," the epitome of that doleful song—which might, by the way, be applied to me:

> On top of old Smoky
> All covered with snow
> I lost my true lover
> For courtin' so slow.

After daylight a cold mist was drifting across the peak, so I didn't linger. The magnificent forests of spruce and fir that once thrived in the area north of Clingmans Dome are now dead, apparently from a combination of disease, fire, air pollution, and possibly other factors. The dead snags still tower above new growth. Very sad.

Newfound Gap, at nearly a mile high in elevation, is the site of the only highway that crosses the Great Smoky Mountains. A memorial there honors the Rockefeller family, which donated much of the land to establish the park. As usual, the area around the big parking lot was crowded with tourists. I got a lonely feeling among all those strangers and didn't linger except to get water at the restroom.

A man at Icewater Spring said, "Just for you to get this far at your age is an accomplishment." Could be! To the north is Charlies Bunion, a clifftop ledge that is rather fearsome. An alternate route goes there, but I decided to keep to the designated Trail.

Beyond is the Sawteeth Range, a narrow ridgetop with steep cliffs on both sides. The terrain is tilted, with vertical bedrock and deep, narrow valleys. When winds cross the Tennessee Valley and are suddenly uplifted thousands of feet, the result is heavy rainfall and violent storms, which expose loose rocks. Whole valleys are sometimes clogged with uprooted and tangled trees. You have to stop to stare at the magnificent scenery, not daring to move without watching your footing. North of the Smokies the terrain is less abrupt, more subdued.

At Pecks Corner, where the trail makes an abrupt turn, there is a small space between a steep slope on the right and on the trail

*Please note that Great Smoky Mountains National Park now prohibits camping outside of the designated shelter system.

A creek on Sugarland Mountain, Great Smoky Mountains National Park

above, a still steeper cliff to the left. With deep darkness very near, it was time to turn in. The shelter proved to be less than a mile away. I stopped there for water and talk.

A side trail leads to the summit of Mount Guyot. It is named for the man who first studied the flora and fauna of the Southern mountains and prepared a map of the area. The map was lost in government files for more than 100 years before it was found by Myron Avery of the Appalachian Trail Conference, and was reproduced through the ATC.

From there the trail slants downward to Davenport Gap and the Pigeon River. The old cable bridge is gone and the crossing is now over a highway bridge.

From the junction I turned aside to the restaurant at Mountain Moma's Kuntry Store & Bunkhouse for a famous Mountain Moma cheeseburger and some ice cream, a welcome change from my spartan diet. There is a washing machine here, much sought after by hikers.

Snowbird Mountain is a rounded dome where the Spanish oak has been replaced by a flight-navigation homing installation. At about mile 250, Max Patch is another dome-shaped peak, but entirely covered with grass. The Trail bypassed it in '48, when cattle were grazing there. The Trail now crosses the open summit, with views in every direction. A cold and lonely wind was blowing, and I hurried across to find a sleeping place below tree line.

That night I awoke to see a bluish ball of light bobbing among the bushes, a will-o'-the-wisp. Some call it fox fire. It broke up and faded, a fragment drifting directly above me.

My morning wake-up call was the rat-a-tat-tat of a pileated wood-pecker getting its breakfast in the solitude of the forest. This is a bird often heard but seldom seen.

The Walnut Mountain Shelter is still standing, saved for the present by sentimental old-timers. Built of chestnut logs, it has been there about 60 years and is still usable.

Lots of blooming laurel, my favorite, highlighted the woods and scented the air on the way to the town of Hot Springs, where the Trail crosses the French Broad River on the highway bridge. The town, with its friendly people and its stores and restaurants, is a

A hiker pauses on Charlies Bunion, Great Smoky Mountains National Park

Earl Shaffer leads the Trail Fest Parade in Hot Springs, North Carolina

Mushrooms along the Trail near Laurel Gorge, Tennessee

favorite with hikers—and its residents love the Trail. Two weeks before the start of my trip, the town had hosted its annual Trail Fest, this time celebrating 50 years of thru-hiking, with me as honored guest. The parade was a lulu, led by four police cars, and it even had a bagpipe band. This time through town, I stopped to visit with Elmer Hall of the Sunnybank Inn, Dan "Wingfoot" Bruce of the Center for Appalachian Trail Studies, and many other "trail people."

North of town the Trail has been relocated along the river and up a steep and crumbly cliff listed in trail data as "Lovers Leap." Definitely a hazardous change, this climb is as scary as any along the Trail. That evening a whip-poor-will sang my lullaby near Rich Mountain Fire Tower.

The Trail now bypasses the fire tower at Camp Creek Bald, where in '48 I slept at the invitation of the lookout. He said he had seen a mountain lion when a light snow was on the ground, and that its print in the snow was as big as a doubled fist. A nearby level area was used as an emergency landing strip during World War II.

About 10 miles to the north, on Big Butt Mountain, are the graves of the Shelton brothers—Union soldiers who were ambushed by Confederates when they tried to visit their homes while on furlough—and their nephew.

I continued through Devil Fork Gap and beyond, along a roaring brook, past a waterfall, to the North Carolina/Tennessee state line, where fragments of fence divide abandoned pastures now covered with flowers.

The old road through Sams Gap has been replaced by a four-lane highway, US 23. People ask about the greatest danger on the Trail. That's easy: crossing a four-lane highway. You wait for the chance to scurry to the median strip, then wait again before crossing the other half. It's a scary experience.

The climb to Big Bald is long and hard on a hot day. The Trail didn't cross the peak 50 years ago. Like Max Patch, it now is covered with grass, and a mountaintop cattle ranch no longer operates there. At the upper level, a strong, cold wind was blowing—no place to linger for the views to the far horizons in every direction. I hurried on and found a place to sleep in the trees below the bald. A stop on top would have been disastrous: A wild thunderstorm made the night a nightmare.

The Smell of the Rain

The smell of the rain comes surging
Out of the shadowed hills,
Filters of vapor purging
The night air of its ills.

Pungent with laden promise
Of cleansing wind and rain,
Often I turn to scent it,
Always to turn again.

I've watched the dry earth filling,
I know its tortured thirst.
I've seen streams dry and barren
And then by floods immersed.

The sun must shine to warm us
But dare not shine too long,
And rain must bring us water
But dare not flow too strong.

And rain can't join with sunshine
To give us perfect weather
For each alone is far too strong
To ever join together.

The Appalachian Trail northbound along Clingmans Dome

At No Business Knob Shelter I stopped for a while to dry out. Toward evening the Trail switchbacked down to the Nolichucky River. As I was turning to cross the highway bridge, voices hailed me from the Nolichucky Hostel. They belonged to some hikers I'd met before. One of them was Dave Donaldson, who had adopted the trail name "Spirit of '48" in honor of my Long Cruise. The proprietor of the hostel, "Uncle Johnny," persuaded me to stay the night and provided me with a steak dinner, bunk, shower, breakfast, and a shuttle to a super-market in the town of Erwin, Tennessee—all for a reasonable charge, about half the usual. He said he had already hosted more than 300 hikers and expected more when the college gang came through. In '48 I had camped by an abandoned house near the river and was serenaded by whip-poor-wills. This area at the Nolichucky River was a favorite village site of the Cherokee Indians.

From the 'Chucky, the Trail trends upward to Curley Maple Gap, where I once met Dorothy Laker, who should be recognized as the first woman to complete a genuine end-to-end trip over the Trail. Dot Laker thru-hiked the Trail twice, the first time almost to the end before anyone took notice. On her second thru-hike, she and I hiked together from Curley Maple Gap to Damascus, Virginia, so I can testify to her hiking ability.

The first woman to hike all the Trail in one season was Mildred Lamb, who later walked many miles on the roads of America as the "Peace Pilgrim." She hiked the southern half of the Trail from the south, then the northern half from the north, an approach now known as a "flip-flop." Doing a flip-flop hike is like going halfway through a tunnel, then exiting and going in the other way. A flip-flop

A lookout atop Mount Cammerer

is necessary for those who can't finish hiking before bad weather in the North stops them. Mildred sent me a series of postcards written so finely that the contents could have filled an ordinary letter. After ending the trip, she visited me at home.

To a lot of people, I probably look like a bum, but a forest worker at Cherry Gap Shelter said to me, "More than half the hikers quit before Damascus, but you'll make it—you have the look." Surely hoped so.

At one point, I fell headlong into a steep erosion gully, coming to a stop with my left cheek against a stone. No serious injuries, just a black eye. A few more inches would have meant a broken neck. During the Long Cruise, I had begun programming myself to use my arms to catch myself when falling, and this reaction has remained ever since. You do what you can to avoid serious injury and depend on your guardian angel for the rest. This time my angel definitely was on duty.

A ruffed grouse hen exploded into flight at my feet, her chicks fluttering and cheeping away. By sunset I was halfway up the climb to Roan Mountain and stopped at a campsite. At the top is the beginning of a long series of open summits and balds that can take a day to hike. Squalls were forming, but always dissipated. Getting stranded on this treeless highland would be serious, but it is a necessary part of the Trail.

At one high point, an eagle came swiftly from the rear, passed within about 50 feet with a shrill scream, its big eye glaring defiantly at me, and plunged out of sight behind some boulders. This encounter was a highlight of my hike. Our national bird is indeed an impressive creature.

Little Shuckstack Mountain and Fontana Lake as seen from Shuckstack Mountain Lookout

41

> *"To a lot of people, I probably look like a bum, but a forest worker at Cherry Gap Shelter said to me, 'More than half the hikers quit before Damascus, but you'll make it—you have the look.'"*

A few minutes later a pair of ravens went off in the same direction but at a much more leisurely pace. Forget-me-nots were in blossom everywhere, but the rhododendron, for which Roan Mountain is famous, had not yet begun blooming.

At twilight I descended into the trees and slept on the Trail itself because I could find no other level spot. The storm that had threatened on Roan Mountain now materialized, making the rocky trail hazardous.

At Dennis Cove Road I turned aside to Kincora Hostel, run by Pat and Bob Peoples, true friends of the Trail. During the night, another storm came by, but it was harmless for a change.

In the morning a friend of Bob's came to interview me for the local paper—the first media contact of many on this Anniversary Trip. I then headed for Laurel Fork Gorge, where a mountain river flows through a deep cleft between two peaks, with the Trail's best waterfall midway. A flood had wrecked much of the Trail in the gorge, but it was still possible to get to the marvelous falls.

When I hiked the Trail in '48, Watauga Dam, close to Hampton, Tennessee, was being built. Now the dam floods much of Watauga Valley, where Daniel Boone and Davy Crockett, as well as other pioneers, had lived. The Trail crosses the top of the dam.

To the north are several game preserves, where use of the chainsaw is not permitted. All cutting must be done with the old crosscut saw.

Laurel Falls in Cherokee National Forest

A meadow on top of Max Patch Bald along the North Carolina/Tennessee border

Dwarf iris, Laurel Falls Gorge, Tennessee

❖ ❖ ❖

A moth on Roan Mountain, Pisgah National Forest, Tennessee

Off the trail about 100 feet is the memorial to Nick Grindstaff in the form of his cabin's lone chimney, which serves as his headstone. Nick lived there as a hermit with a rattlesnake as his companion after his sweetheart married another man.

I stopped to sleep 5 miles from Damascus. A thunderstorm came at night, then another farther along the way, and a third while I was in town—nature gone wild.

Stormy Moonlight

The half-moon is high at the zenith ringed
Around with a halo of silver light.
The storm-bound horizon is amply winged
With ragged titanics of somber might,
And both are a menace to peaceful night.

The moon is a ghost ship on waters gray,
The clouds are the billows, white-fringed with foam,
Consuming the sky in a mad array
Of fleeting allurement and silver gloam,
And quicksilver visions that speak of home.

Though moonlight be lonely and pathos-filled
And etched on a stormy malignant sky,
The touch of its beauty remains instilled
With unallayed urgence to rise and fly.

The Appalachian Trail heads north toward Big Bald Mountain in Pisgah National Forest

An old apple tree is silhouetted at Devil Fork Gap, Pisgah National Forest

Sunrise from Rich Mountain in Cherokee National Forest

Next page: *The Appalachian Trail heads north up Hump Mountain in North Carolina*

Mountain Fever

I wish I could find a mountain to climb upon today,
A mountain of sprawling timber where the air is crisp and cool,
Whose crest is a hard-won summit from which shadows shrink away
As doubts that must be deleted in nature's forthright school.

I wish I could climb a mountain so my blood could throb with joy
And the boundless sense of freedom so inherent with the sky,
And fling to the purgin' elements the thoughts that would destroy
A love of the windswept ledges and the untamed eagle's cry.

I wish I could loose my spirit to the moon among the trees
Or out to the tawny sunset on the ridges far away,
Or drift on the pine-drenched whispers of the restless canopies
That mantle the mighty mountains in their velvet purple gray.

I wish I could stand unhindered on the jutting boulder piles
That reach to an awful summit as a finely balanced tower,
And spread for the ardent climber vast and panoramic miles
That testify so mutely of the earth's vast latent power.

I wish I could climb a mountain so my pulsing blood could flow
Once more to the thrill and tumult of the clear untrammeled air,
And out on the ageless monarchs sense again as long ago
The peace and the deep contentment that are so abundant there.

Damascus, Virginia *to* Pearisburg, Virginia

The town of Damascus, Virginia, which is approximately one-quarter of the way to the northern end of the Trail, was much smaller in '48 and I had passed through on May Day almost unnoticed. This time many people greeted me. Damascus claims to be the friendliest town along the Appalachian Trail, and it probably is, although Hot Springs, North Carolina, also can claim that honor.

The church-run hostel in Damascus is called "The Place." Many hikers were there, probably waiting for a break in the weather. An Associated Press correspondent came there to interview me, and she included some of the other hikers, too.

From Damascus the Trail is on contour level, cut along the side of a ridge, with no appreciable changes in elevation. It is also narrow, almost rock-free, so a mis-step could mean a long, sliding fall. Such sections are hiker-friendly, however, because you might pass a spring.

Cold spring water that comes up from underground is generally safe to drink. Many hikers carry a filter gadget, which I do not trust. When in doubt, I add a smidgen of vinegar, which also minimizes the chance of a cold or sore throat and digestive upset. It must be the yellow vinegar, which is made from apples and needs no sterilization. The white kind has been distilled and is worthless.*

A tent city during Trail Days in Damascus, Virginia

In '48 the original Trail in southwest Virginia went eastward from Damascus as far as Galax on the New River before turning north, mostly on dirt roads, to the vicinity of Roanoke, where it turned west to circle the city. The new off-road route goes north and west and finally rejoins the original route west of Roanoke. The Roan Mountain and Mount Rogers relocations also were added, so the route from Watauga Dam south of Damascus to Catawba Mountain west of Roanoke is mostly new, except for sections near Damascus and some of the route along the Tennessee/North Carolina line. These relocations were in place at the time of my second thru-hike, my '65 Autumn Stroll. During that trip, about one-third of the Trail was different. I decided to take another look.

Leaving Damascus, the Trail follows a roaring stream. Then came Whitetop Mountain—a long, hard climb—and Elk Garden, before Mount Rogers, the highest peak in Virginia at 5,729 feet. Its flat top is boggy, but I side-trailed there just so I could say I had been there.

Many day hikers were out, and one of them stopped. He had brought a copy of the book I wrote to document my Long Cruise, *Walking With Spring*, in hopes he would meet me for an autograph. In exchange he gave me a Swiss Army pocketknife, which I carried for the rest of the hike.

*Contact the Center for Appalachian Trail Studies (p. 9) or the Appalachian Trail Conference (p. 126) for recommended water treatment methods.

Opposite: *Wilburn Ridge, Mount Rogers National Recreation Area, Virginia*

51

A fungus-covered snag arches over the Appalachian Trail on Locust Mountain

The Trail passes rocky meadows with feral horses and ponies and grazing cattle. I made it to Old Orchard Shelter before stopping for the night. In this area I saw white rhododendron—the first to bloom—and several deer and a hopping rabbit. We were in the midst of a spell of wet weather, with chilly fog.

Lullaby Song of the Rain

Lullaby song of the raindrops,
Shutter my eyes in sleep,
Croon your melodious rhapsody,
Lull me to slumbers deep.

Sing to the men in the pup tents
Only a mild refrain,
For pup tents aren't too waterproof
So please don't really rain.

Only a sprinkle in nighttime,
Pour if you must by day.
Bring to the earth refreshment
But please don't come to stay.

Those who live out in a pup tent
Always prefer it dry.
Lullaby song of the raindrops,
Whimper but don't you cry.

Bring to us solace from heartache,
Patience and poignancy.
We who are far from our homeland,
Teach us your constancy.

The Trail in Wilburn Ridge Cave, Mount Rogers National Recreation Area

Black-eyed Susans decorate the Trail near Atkins, Virginia

At the US 11 highway crossing I was able to get short-term supplies at a gas station. Knot Maul Branch Shelter is named for the knotted clubs that loggers used to drive wedges. Trees in the area were the source of the hard knots that made these tools.

Sometimes the Trail crosses hay fields; there were no pole-centered stacks as in '48, just bales. In a pasture, two young bulls were sparring. Herds of steers would bunch and follow. Some of the herds had unbelievably big bulls—fortunately not aggressive. Many of the fences had stiles to help hikers crawl over. This section of the Trail was recently relocated from roads. Please, whoever's in charge, put it back the way it was!

I didn't go down to Davis Farm Campsite. Those who did said they met up with a big rattlesnake.

I side-trailed to the impressive Dismal Creek Falls and then continued on to stop and meditate at Wapiti Shelter. About 15 miles up the Trail, the Angels Rest vista overlooks Pearisburg. When I stopped there to rest, an eagle came in, wings spread, to land. It spotted me and plunged by, about 10 feet away. You can't realize how big and impressive one of these eagles is until you see it up close.

At Sugar Run Gap, a sign on a tree said, "Earl, go down to Woodshole. Tillie's breakfast is famous, Tim and Gary." Those two had passed that way a few days ahead of me. They were right about the breakfast!

The descent from Angels Rest to Pearisburg, Virginia, is twisty and treacherous. In town is the church-run Holy Family Hospice, which is popular with hikers. At the shoe repair shop, I replaced my unsatisfactory footgear with a new pair of workboots.

Song of Early Summer

Somewhere away from streets and telephones,
Under the trees upon a mountainside,
Cool water seeps between moss-covered stones
Down a ravine where salamanders hide.

Little Wolf Creek in Washington-Jefferson National Forest

Next page: *Dawn view from Whitetop Mountain, Virginia*

Moonlighted Clouds

*White clouds like piles of eiderdown
On yonder hills recline,
Lit by a moon that shines so bright
That few stars dare to shine.*

*While over all a silence deep
That blends into the sheen,
Majestic in simplicity,
What can this silence mean?*

*It means that God is on his throne
Creating pictures fair,
That man in all his ignorance
May witness if he care.*

*Yet while men rant and rave and seek
To do as they may please,
The moon keeps shining peacefully
On clouds and hills and trees.*

Pearisburg, Virginia
to Rockfish Gap, Virginia

After Pearisburg, I hiked a 10-mile stretch of rimrock that overlooks the valley. Later, along a straight ridge, an eagle came, its wings set, riding the wind, not moving a feather, and disappeared to the rear. Then a big doe stood like a statue and watched as I passed.

Hiking through grasslands, I came to the Keffer Oak, said to be the fattest tree along the Trail, at more than 18 feet around. (Some consider the Dover Oak near Pawling, New York, to be the Trail's largest tree.) It stands in a bowl-shaped depression in which a pool of water had formed when I was there, which might explain its long survival. I slept within sight of it on the ridge.

Farther on is the memorial to Audie Murphy, the most decorated veteran of World War II. He died in a plane crash nearby. Then I met a stretch of sidehill that might be called "Drapery Trail" because it sags between rocks and trees. At times the Trail is on narrow rock ledges, with now and then a gigantic boulder barring the way so you must scramble to pass.

The Tyro grocery store

The next day I came to the Dragons Tooth, twin slabs of rock jutting from a cliff. A new relocation has taken the Trail down a rocky cliff, a real danger zone. One woman fell, spent five days in a hospital, and had both legs taped.

About a week ago I began feeling in my left lung a dull ache, which moved to the side, but suddenly I began to breathe freely again. I feared that the shortness of breath I had at first blamed on old age might have been a collapsed lung. Whatever it was, it must have miraculously cured itself. The human body certainly is a remarkable creation.

The Boy Scout Shelter is probably the shabbiest—and surely the longest—lean-to along the Trail, but it was certainly a welcome haven after a long, hot day. The spring was dry, however, and my water supply was zero.

An early start took me to Catawba Mountain Shelter, where the spring was a puddle. Soon the Trail led through a region of enormous square-shaped boulders to the summit of MacAfee Knob and a half-circle view of the Catawba Valley and distant peaks against towering cloud banks.

Opposite: *A field of wild bergamot in the Sinking Creek Valley, Virginia*

Valley of Sunset

Valley that lies in the shadow of sunset,
Sweeping on outward to meet with the sky,
Gray in the gloaming, your cloak is of velvet,
Drawing subsistence from beauty on high.

Far in the vanguard your vagrants go roaming,
Borne on the path of the vanishing sun,
Lost to the beauty of you in the gloaming,
Swept on the tide of a battle begun.

Silver your mantle of dew in the morning,
Green as the new leaves your verdure at noon,
Spun with the essence of love dreams forlorning
Under the spell of a whimsical moon.

Valley that lies in the path of the sky,
Who could more vividly miss you than I?

A few miles farther on are the Tinker Cliffs, with the Trail blazed along the edge. There, I met a hiker who gave me a pint of water from his own scant supply. Food is important for hikers, but water is more so. The only thing more important is air.

After several miles I met my nephew David and his daughter Maggie on the Trail. The other hiker had told them of my problem and they had brought water. I drank two quarts without stopping. David and Maggie hiked with me to the road at Daleville, Virginia, then started for home in Ohio. David said my brother John also was in the area trying to intercept me, but had missed me by a few minutes at the Boy Scout Shelter. John had been contacted by NBC's *Today Show* and was trying to arrange a meeting.

Dogwood and redbud trees in bloom near Dragons Tooth

Sunset from Spy Rock

Trillium and large-flowered bellwort in the Thunder Ridge Wilderness

US 11 marks the way of the ancient Indian war path between the tribes of the North and South. At another gas station, I obtained more short-term supplies.

The Trail meets the Blue Ridge Parkway near Roanoke, where the Trail skirts the city from Bent Mountain. The parkway southwest of Roanoke replaced the old Appalachian Trail route, which swept past the incomparable Pinnacles of Dan, a pyramidal peak bounded on three sides by the Dan River. North of Roanoke, the Trail crosses the tops of the mountains. The Blue Ridge Parkway winds through the gaps, with many trail crossings along the way. This is the least remote section of the Trail, continuing through Shenandoah National Park.

At one of the crossings, John, his daughter Robin, and her son Trey caught up with me to set up a meeting with the NBC crew in Shenandoah National Park. They brought food and water, which was very welcome.

The Trail still crosses Apple Orchard Mountain, now topped by a flight-navigation homing transmitter. It is difficult to believe that this mountaintop was once an apple orchard.

At Thunder Hill Shelter the Washingtons, trail friends and former thru-hikers, gave me some snacks and drinks. When I stretched out to relax, Mrs. Washington exclaimed, "Don't move while I get my camera!" In the morning I hitchhiked to Glasgow. Hitching is difficult in Virginia, so it took most of the day.

Another couple I met had come back to finish a hike begun the year before. The husband said that his wife, ahead of us on the Trail, had stepped right over a coiled rattlesnake without seeing it. She was lucky. The second hiker in line is usually the one bitten. Snakes are now rare along the Trail. The many hikers seem to have chased them away. Eight-inch boots and long pants are the best protection against snakes. Long pants also protect against insects, sunburn, and poison ivy.

A long series of switchbacks took me to an overlook showing the James River snaking its way through the Blue Ridge Mountains toward the Atlantic Ocean. All rivers south of this point flow westward. From now on, all rivers would be flowing eastward.

I passed the spot where "Little Ottie" Powell's body was found in 1891. He had strayed 7 miles from a valley schoolhouse. He was four years and seven months old when he died. Some say his ghost haunts the nearby Punchbowl Shelter.

I passed the site of Bluff Mountain Tower, an old fire tower no longer there, on an easy trail to Pedlar Dam, the water supply for Lynchburg. The rickety old bridge that I remembered had been replaced.

A thunderstorm came at night to Brown Mountain Creek Shelter. About 7 miles farther on, Cold Mountain is much like the balds to the south.

From Tar Jacket Ridge, an open summit designated as "safe from development," the Alleghenies are on the horizon to the west. Ten miles up the Trail, Spy Rock, a rock dome with a miniature lake on the top, was a vantage point for Confederates during the Civil War. In '48 the relocation of the Trail between Spy Rock and The Priest was projected but not complete, so I proceeded by compass through this trailless area for several miles to The Priest. Back then there was a sign near Spy Rock pointing to a road crossing.

This time Ed Williams met me at the road crossing. On the doors of his truck he had painted "Trail Angel," and he provided me with food and drinks. Later I passed Humpback Rocks on the way to Rockfish Gap. I stopped at a motel to eat an enormous burger and was trying to phone John when Ed drove up. He said I could call from his home and stay overnight. He was insistent so there I was, being fed baked trout, fresh tomatoes, and other goodies, and I was able to call John to finalize the meeting with the TV crew in Shenandoah National Park. Ed and Mary Ann Williams acted as though I was favoring them with my presence. Breakfast consisted of eggs and bacon, with all the trimmings. Mary Ann gave me boiled eggs and cornbread to take along, and Ed drove me back to Rockfish Gap, where I signed for a permit to hike through Shenandoah National Park.

This tree has grown around an old Appalachian Trail sign

A frog near Piney River, Washington-Jefferson National Forest

Next page: *A Virginia sunset blazes the sky above Brushy Mountain*

Midsummer Gone

When katydids chant, midsummer is gone
Into a limbo of lengthening night.
They tell us that autumn is coming on
The nocturnal stage, illumined by light
Of fireflies and stars and the Milky Way,
And boreal lights that flutter and flare.
For someone alone and haplessly fey
They tell of the time when branches are bare.
A cuckoo complains in the humid dark,
A screech owl was shrilling an hour ago.
And maybe we'll hear, if we listen…Hark!
The murmur of waters that barely flow.
Summer is with us but will not be long,
When katydids offer their rasping song.

Rockfish Gap, Virginia *to the* Maryland/Pennsylvania border

Shenandoah National Park differs from Great Smoky Mountains National Park, as the mountain range here is very dominant, rising abruptly from the adjacent valley. Families living on little farms in the hollows were moved out, and the vacated areas were allowed to grow back into forest.

At a road crossing beyond Blackrock Hut, I again met Ed and Mary Ann Williams, who were passing out homemade ice cream to hikers. While I was there, three park rangers stopped to talk. They told me that hikers were often seen along the Skyline Drive, apparently bypassing parts of the Trail. At the first conference of the "Two Thousand Milers," the committee on authenticating thru-hikers was asked what verification, such as a day-by-day report, was required. They replied, "Oh, we take their word for it."

I stopped at a store at Lewis Mountain Campground. No hiker can pass up the chance to get food. It's a compulsion.

On the way to Bearfence Mountain Hut I met a group of Mennonites, easily identified by their distinctively plain clothing. At the hut I met brother John, his wife Lois, the *Today Show* TV crew, and reporter Michael Vitez and photographer Michael Perez from *The Philadelphia Inquirer*. When the TV crew commented on my age, my reply was, "Age is only the number of years you have lived"—some people look young when

◆ ◆ ◆

Pink azaleas in Shenandoah National Park

◆ ◆ ◆

they're old, and others look old when they're young. I spent two nights at the hut to accommodate the media, and the newspaper reporter and photographer tagged along to Big Meadows Campground before turning back. In the afternoon, I passed Franklin Cliffs and Marys Rock, an ancient rock named for a pioneer wife.

My eye swelled after a bite from an insect—I had waited too long before using my headnet. Insects are the bane of a thru-hiker's existence on the Trail. Long-sleeved pants and shirts provide the best protection, although most hikers wear shorts and suffer for it.

Much of the scenery in the park was blurred by haze and fog, caused mainly by air pollution. Many trees have died, as they did in the Smokies. The Byrds Nests are stone lean-tos along the Trail. These picnic facilities have no bunks, and camping isn't allowed.

By sunset I was at the visitor center at Elkwallow Gap. The restaurant and store were closed, so I slept in the woods nearby and bought supplies and ate in the morning. Some stretches of trail in the park are surprisingly remote.

North of the park boundary is the Jim and Molly Denton Shelter. If Jim could see this "Hilton of the Appalachian Trail," he wouldn't believe his eyes! It has a furnished patio, cooking pavilion, and shower, with immaculate grounds.

Opposite: *Azaleas in bloom beside the Appalachian Trail in Virginia*

Sky Meadows State Park, Virginia

A four-foot blacksnake was on the trail near the Linden Road crossing. The few miles past Rod Hollow Shelter are nothing from nowhere—up and down, in and out, back and forth—a maze that would drive a compass crazy, especially on such a hot day. The side trail to Blackburn Appalachian Trail Center is poorly marked and I missed it. At David Lesser Memorial Shelter a reporter from the *Baltimore Sun*, Ernie Imhoff, was waiting and he tagged along with me. Bruce Dunlavy, a recent thru-hiker with the trail name of "Ishmael," met me at a road crossing and hiked with me to Harpers Ferry, West Virginia.

> "'Age is only the number of years you have lived'—some people look young when they're old, and others look old when they're young."

The Appalachian Trail Conference headquarters is located in Harpers Ferry; at about mile 1,000, the town is considered by many thru-hikers to be the Trail's psychological halfway point (the original halfway point was Center Point Knob, Pennsylvania). Laurie Potteiger and other ATC staff members had arranged a press conference, followed by a party with a specially decorated cake. Bill Bowden, a reporter/photographer for the *York Daily Record*, the morning paper in my hometown, was at the press conference, and he and Laurie hiked with me to US 40.

At Harpers Ferry Hostel after the party, I stretched out flat on the ground to rest for an hour before registering to stay overnight.

Longtime Trail worker Thurston Griggs, who is two years older than I, met me at Gathland State Park for a sentimental talk. That night I slept near the I-70 footbridge that spans six lanes near Boonsboro, Maryland. The original Washington Monument, built by the people of Boonsboro in 1827, stands in Washington Monument State Park.

The view south from Mary's Rock, Shenandoah National Park, Virginia

Farther along, a side trail leads to Devils Racecourse, a long, flat area of rocks where a stream can be heard flowing beneath. In '48 this remarkable place was on the Trail.

Near the Mason–Dixon Line, I had a nasty fall on a relocated portion of the Trail that now crosses boulder terrain, but escaped with no serious injuries. Pen Mar County Park has been greatly improved since '48. A ranger there took me and other hikers to a store and back.

To Pennsylvania

When the leaves begin a-changin'
And the corn is turnin' gold,
When the polecats start a-rangin'
'Cause the nights are gettin' cold,
When the harvest moon's a-shinin'
On the meadows wet with dew,
There's an exile who's a-pinin'
To be comin' back to you.

The historic Chesapeake and Ohio Canal in Maryland

Looking down on Harpers Ferry, West Virginia, from Maryland Heights in Maryland

Next page: *The Potomac River as seen from the Weverton Cliffs, Maryland*

Rausch Creek Ramble

Down from the mine-pocked mountain crest,
Twisting and spilling through the glen,
The crystal waters ever quest
Toward the mother sea again.

The laurel and the evergreen
In tangled thickets dipping low
Obscure and isolate the scene
Where only venturous hikers go.

And one deep pool, the best of all,
Pale green, foamy, and icy cold,
Between two bits of waterfall,
Wondrously lovely to behold.

Rausch Creek has drawn us back into
The sylvan ways of wandering,
Where laurel clusters bloom anew
And brimming waters dance and sing.

What do the water voices say
To those who pause and ponder there?
"The woodlands teem with the spell of May.
The charm of spring is everywhere."

Maryland/Pennsylvania border
to the Delaware River

My first stop in Pennsylvania was at Antietam Shelter, near the historic battle site. The Trail crosses US 30 at Caledonia State Park. During the Civil War, the Confederate Army under General Lee marched along this highway to the Battle of Gettysburg and withdrew by the same route. An old friend, Keith Francis, chanced to come by and drove me down the highway to a store, where he treated me to ice cream.

The stretch of trail from here to Center Point Knob is very familiar to me. During the 1930s, my younger brother Evan and I hiked this section, my first time ever on the Appalachian Trail. On my Long Cruise in '48, a lifelong friend, Woody Baughman, was with me here. Three years later I accompanied hiker Bill Hall on his "almost thru-hike." And many years after that, a few weeks before starting my Anniversary Trip, brother John and I hiked this same section to see whether I could still handle a packload after a long layoff.

This time, at Birch Run Shelters, some reporters were waiting and tagged along to Pine Grove Furnace Store. There, they dared me to join the "Half-Gallon Club," a thru-hiker tradition, by providing a half-gallon of ice cream and waiting to see if I could eat it all—which I did easily, and I was tempted to shock them by asking for more.

◆◆◆

The Thelma Marks Shelter, built by Earl Shaffer

◆◆◆

Beyond Pine Grove Furnace State Park a few miles is Pole Steeple, a ridgetop outcropping of quartzite looming above Laurel Lake, a flooded ore pit used for swimming and fishing. Across the valley is a spot that is especially memorable for me, the site of my first overnight stay in the mountains:

THE VALE MICHAUX
A mountain valley girt with laurel green,
A farling place when I was seventeen,
A dawning place for tendencies to roam
Beyond the lesser rolling hills of home.
My first lone camp was in the vale Michaux
On Holly Mountain many years ago.

Bruce Dunlavy, this time accompanied by fellow thru-hiker George Anderson, joined me for several miles. By evening I was at Hunters Run, just 3 or 4 miles from my present home near Gettysburg. I hitchhiked there to sleep in my own bed, and hitched back early in the morning with a local Boy Scout leader.

The morning hike took me to Whiskey Spring, where a long-ago logger kept his whiskey cold in a recess behind the spring. Another few miles took me to Center Point Knob, which I still consider the approximate halfway point, in spite of the many changes to the Trail.

Boiling Springs—one of the largest springs in Pennsylvania—is about 3 miles north on Yellow Breeches Creek. The town is built around the lake, where the tremendous volume of water surfaces.

Opposite: *A hiker on the Trail through Boiling Springs, Pennsylvania*

Next to the lake is the ATC Regional Office, where a group, including a local TV crew, had gathered to welcome me. The festivities also included watermelon-eating.

From here the Trail crosses the Cumberland Valley on Ironstone Ridge to Blue Mountain and Cove Mountain, one of the few perfect V-shaped mountains on earth. The north arm of Cove Mountain leads to Hawk Rock, a high outcropping overlooking the Susquehanna River, the town of Duncannon, Pennsylvania, and the valley of the Juniata River.

Indian Lookout

Peaceful and calm flows the broad Susquehanna
Studded with boulders and flanked by the bluffs.
Breezes like shafts from the bow of Diana
Ripple the surface in whimsical puffs.

The rock like a sentinel, grim and foreboding,
Rearing in majesty over the trees,
Stands as a watcher, alert and imposing,
Vested with dignity, always at ease.

There lurked the warriors in days of the ancients,
Guarding the ford that lies off to the north,
Trying to equal the old boulder's patience,
Knowing that someday the foe would come forth.

Many a tale could that old rock be telling,
Legends of days when the river ran red,
Keeping its vigil in silence instead.

Conococheague Creek in Caledonia State Park, Pennsylvania

View from Hawk Rock in Pennsylvania

Of necessity, the Trail goes through Duncannon, which provides stores and eating places. My stop was at a supermarket, where a newspaper displayed—you guessed it—a picture of me. I carefully refrained from wearing my pith helmet, so no one noticed me.

On Duncannon's north end, an island at the junction of the Susquehanna and Juniata Rivers was a powwow meeting place for the Iroquois and other tribes. A large mound was located on the island but was destroyed when the Clarks Ferry Bridge across the Susquehanna was constructed. This bridge provides the river crossing for the Appalachian Trail.

Beyond the Susquehanna River the Trail traverses Peters Mountain for about 15 miles before crossing Clarks Valley. Near the valley road a young lady with a big pack and a gigantic hound dog was wary of sleeping so near the road. I was able to direct her to a spring and campsite farther up the mountain.

Rausch Creek at Rausch Gap, Pennsylvania

My bed was under tall pines at the site of the former Stony Mountain Fire Tower, where the Horse-Shoe Trail meets the Appalachian Trail. From this northern end point, the Horse-Shoe Trail leads to Valley Forge. Beyond the junction is St. Anthony's Wilderness, as shown on an ancient map. A stage road leads through terrain as remote as you can find in the central Appalachians.

The Trail leaves the stage road at Rausch Gap, site of an abandoned town that once was a thriving coal mining community. The shelter there is nicknamed the "Halfway Hilton." It even has running water from an uphill spring.

Wanderer's Quest

Somewhere on this earth there's a valley,
A valley that's peaceful and fair,
Where everyone's friendly and all quickly rally
If danger or trouble comes there.

Where no one is selfish and no one is cruel
And greed for wealth is unknown,
Where no one's a genius, no one a fool,
And only true kindness is shown.

A clear stream is flowing between lofty ranges
Well timbered with maple and pine,
A vista serene where life never changes,
Where leisure and peace will be mine.

Long have I sought for that lone hidden valley
But always have sought it in vain,
Yet each disappointment will cause me to rally
And eagerly seek it again.

Farther along, at Green Point, is one of the longest road walks on the Appalachian Trail (now relocated). Plans for a state park have kept the Trail route in limbo. The Trail crosses Swatara Creek on a historic iron bridge. That night I slept at William Penn Shelter, named after the founder of Pennsylvania.

In the morning John, this time accompanied by our oldest brother, Dan, intercepted me at the PA 501 road crossing and drove me to a store for food supplies. Pilger Ruh (Pilgrim's Rest), where Moravian missionaries stopped on their way to visit Indians, is now on a side trail. A spring there is called Ludwig's Brunne. Another unusual place is Showers Steps, constructed down a mountainside by Lloyd Showers, an early trail-builder in Pennsylvania. This boulder stairway of 500 steps leads to a road in the valley.

Farther along the Trail is the site of Fort Dietrich Snyder, one of the frontier forts built under the supervision of Benjamin Franklin during the French and Indian War; farther yet is Port Clinton, Pennsylvania, a town on the Schuylkill River near the birthplace of Daniel Boone (when he was a teenager his family moved to North Carolina). Ten miles beyond is The Pinnacle, a fine viewpoint for the Lehigh Valley toward Philadelphia. My stay at the Allentown Hiking Club Shelter was rainy, just as it was 50 years ago.

George Outerbridge Shelter is named for one of the first hikers to cover the whole Trail in sections. After crossing the Lehigh River, at Lehigh Gap the Trail ascends a steep and treacherous slope that really ought to be bypassed. Beyond is the dreariest stretch on the entire Trail, several miles of desolation caused by fumes from a zinc refinery no longer in operation.

Eastern Pennsylvania is notorious for its stumble stones—small, flat stones wedged vertically for miles at a time. Hiking on this terrain causes foot and leg problems, and Trail relocations over boulder "obstacle courses" add to the misery.

PA 33 at Wind Gap is the usual dangerous four-lane "dodge-and-run." Beyond Wind Gap a group of people carrying nothing begged me for water I didn't have. Ten minutes later a man came along wearing nothing. I hope the insects take advantage of such outrageous behavior!

Kirkridge Shelter is the last one northbound in Pennsylvania. It's near a private retreat, and water is available from a spigot.

The Trail looms high above the Delaware Water Gap, with Tammany Mountain directly across in New Jersey. The mountain is named for a Delaware Indian chief who signed the treaty with William Penn. According to legend the Delawares called the valley to the north (a former lake) "Minisink," meaning "the water is gone." The twisted strata of Tammany Mountain indicate the water's recession. In '48 I had to go 5 miles to Portland Bridge to cross the Delaware River, but now a highway bridge spans the river at Delaware Water Gap.

Sunrise from Chimney Rocks, Pennsylvania

Next page: *The Susquehanna River and Halifax Hamlet from Peters Mountain, Pennsylvania*

Hobo

Footloose and fancy free, always a-roaming,
Here at the dawning, there at the gloaming,
You're always drifting, you have no abode.
Why do you wander, knight of the road?

Is it the wanderlust makes you move on?
You're here today, tomorrow you're gone.
Is it the passionate lure to be free,
Or is it the lure of the places you see?

Or is it a different virulent cause
That keeps you moving with scarcely a pause,
Someone or something that caused you to roam,
That makes you averse to friends and a home?

You're friendless and lonely, yet always aloof,
The ground is your bed, the sky is your roof,
Uneasy and restless with little to say,
You pause for a time, then go on your way.

You're a rolling stone on the trails that wind
To the last far reaches of all mankind.
Ceaselessly drifting, you haven't a home.
Why are you destined to endlessly roam?

Delaware River *to the* New York/Connecticut border

Beyond Tammany Mountain is Sunfish Pond, the first glacial pond the south-to-north hiker meets on the Trail. From now on, such natural lakes are seen frequently.

The Delaware Indians and their neighboring tribes were gradually squeezed between the settlers and the Iroquois and eventually retreated westward. One stayed behind. The real-life last-of-the-Mohicans died in his wickiup on Kittatinny Mountain.

Much of the Trail in New Jersey has been relocated to rocky terrain. Once I met a group that had stopped while a boy was examined for a possible broken leg. Later, at a road crossing, I went to a house for water and was told that a girl had come out of the woods to get help for her friend, who had fallen among rocks. It took a rescue crew five hours to get her off the mountain. The Trail is much rougher now than it was in '48. Those responsible say they are providing challenges. But is it a challenge when you have no choice?

At High Point State Park headquarters some reporters met me and went along with me to High Point before turning back. From there the Trail turns eastward along the New Jersey/New York state line.

At twilight I came to a no-longer-operating sod farm. The topsoil must have been deep; the removal of successive layers of turf grown for use as instant lawn had resulted in deep, swampy pits and scraggly growth. Now the Walkill National Wildlife Preserve, the farm was not on the Trail in '48.

Hoping for a better place to sleep, I hurried on. Finally, in desperation, I bedded down on the abandoned access road. During the night a swarm of mosquitoes was buzzing outside my head net until some bats came and swooped low to feast on the pests.

Fingerboard Shelter, Harriman State Park, New York

Much of this state line route has been relocated, except for the section across Wawayanda Mountain. Near Greenwood Lake, New York, the Trail turns north. In Palisades Interstate Park, relocations now take the Trail over a series of rock piles, again in an effort to make the hike more challenging.

Harriman State Park, New York's second-largest park, is different, with more open woodland and varied plant life. Somehow I got turned around and was going in the wrong direction when fellow hikers "Boo Boo" and "Yogi," two brothers from the Ozarks, came along and, thankfully, turned me back.

In this area is the famous "Lemon Squeezer," a narrow cleft between boulders. Fingerboard Shelter, where a raccoon harassed me in '48, is still there but is deteriorating.

Opposite: *Delaware Water Gap from the shoulder of Mt. Tammany, New Jersey*

Fall color encircling Island Lake, Harriman State Park, New York

Bear Mountain State Park, about 25 miles north of New York City and adjacent to the Hudson River, contains the first few miles of trail built specifically for the Appalachian Trail in the 1920s. The crossing on the bridge in the town of Bear Mountain, New York, is just beyond the lowest point on the Trail, almost sea level. In '48 it cost me a five-cents toll. This time a violent rainstorm caught me halfway and darkness surrounded me before I could reach the Friary (Graymoor Spiritual Life Center), a deluxe church retreat a few miles to the east. An unhappy night in the wet woods ensued, but I stopped at the retreat to get drinking water in the morning. A line from Samuel Taylor Coleridge's *The Rime of the Ancient Mariner* came to mind: "Water water every where, nor any drop to drink."

The Turning Leaves

The summer is lush and warm.
Leaves flourish everywhere,
Watered by thunderstorm,
Heated by sunny glare
Until the autumnal
Touches of frost, and then
A color carnival,
Defying brush or pen,
Until the leaves at last,
Turning brittle and brown,
By wintry winds harassed
Go swiftly sailing down.

The Trail heading north through the "Lemon Squeezer" in New York

Autumn reflections in Little Dam Lake, New York

◆ ◆ ◆

Fall leaves along the Appalachian Trail in New York

New York's Little Dam Lake is a bird sanctuary for a variety of species

"The Trail is much rougher now than it was in '48. Those responsible say they are providing challenges. But is it a challenge when you have no choice?"

In 1948 a good portion of the Trail in eastern New York followed roads, but most of it has been relocated. From this area 50 years ago, I sent my first message to the Appalachian Trail Conference meeting in Fontana Village, North Carolina, to report my thru-hike. I figured unless something drastic occurred the success of my hike was inevitable, and I ought to let my presence be known. On a sheet of paper I noted the date of my departure from the original southern terminus of the Trail in Georgia, Mount Oglethorpe, and the estimated date of arrival at Katahdin. I also sketched a likeness of the Pinnacles of Dan and wrote below it what I still consider my "theme song":

> *The flowers bloom, the wild songbirds sing*
> *And though it sun or rain,*
> *I walk the mountain tops with Spring*
> *From Georgia north to Maine.*

The message was received at Fontana Village, but it was not seriously considered because a thru-hike was thought to be impossible at the time, so it was discarded.

At a road crossing, I caught a passing bus for a ride to Pawling, New York, for supplies but had a long walk back to the Trail. Farther on is the Appalachian Trail Station, where a train stops for hikers to go to New York City on weekends. Who wants to go for a Broadway show?

At Webatuck Shelter a group of people, including a local reporter, had gathered to greet me. Someone had even brought food for a party!

Next page: *Canopus Lake in Clarence Fahnestock State Park, New York*

Fitzgerald Falls in New York

End of Autumn

When the summer is in its heyday
And the shadowy breezes blow
To cool us according to whimsy
And make us think kindly of snow,

We obviously have forgotten
How deadly the snow wind can feel
When warmth is entirely forsaken
And the winter is starkly real.

New York/Connecticut border *to the* Massachusetts/Vermont border

Near Wingdale, New York, the Trail crosses into Connecticut. Beyond is The River Walk, an easy stroll along the turbulent Housatonic River for several miles with no buildings along the way—an almost wilderness where it's least expected. The St. Johns Ledges are more suitable for rock climbing than backpacking. The stone steps are high, causing off-balancing on the way up and severe shock to the knees on the way down. This route was not on the Trail in '48 and shouldn't be now, at least with the stone steps.

About 20 miles farther on, the historic iron bridge over the Housatonic River is the same type as the one that crosses Swatara Creek in Pennsylvania. At Lower Cobble Road, a water spigot is located near a large stone cross in a cemetery. Water is at a premium this year, so I carry a pair of quart bottles.

I slept at Brassie Brook Lean-to, then summited Bear Mountain, with its stone tower on top. Sages Ravine, which is located near the Connecticut/Massachusetts state line, lies just beyond the mountain. I found its waterfalls and pools to be as beautiful as ever and just as popular with artists. Mount Everett is steep and rocky but offers views from the summit. My overnight stop was at the Glen Brook Lean-to.

A salamander makes its way across the forest floor

At South Egremont, Massachusetts, brothers John and Dan, along with their wives Lois and Betty, met me for a planned visit with friends, the Vinings—and a welcome supper including old-fashioned stew. In the morning Mrs. Vining took me to meet her neighbor, Mrs. Kellogg, a generous contributor to the Appalachian Trail Conference who was anxious to meet me. So she got her wish. She is at least 90 years old and a fine lady.

After the visits and more interviews with reporters, I got only as far as the Tom Leonard Lean-to before dark that day, about 10 miles up the Trail and approximately 1,500 miles from Springer Mountain. Temperatures were dropping with the change of seasons, and would continue to do so as I moved north toward higher elevations in New Hampshire and Maine. I realized it would be a race with time to finish before winter set in.

The remaining thru-hikers—about 10 percent of the starters—are facing the same outlook. Most have been on the Trail for weeks or even months longer than I. They marvel that I'm still among them. The reason is simple: Just don't quit. Brother Dan tells people it takes only one word to describe me: "stubborn."

I went to Tyringham, Massachusetts, which is now bypassed, then back to the Trail and on to scenic Benedict Pond. I stayed

Opposite: *The Housatonic River*

Wood fern on the bank of the Housatonic River

The beautiful Luna moth is one of many creatures found along the Trail

◆ ◆ ◆

Angel hair ferns along the Appalachian Trail

"Temperatures were dropping with the change of seasons, and would continue to do so as I moved north toward higher elevations in New Hampshire and Maine. I realized it would be a race with time to finish before winter set in."

overnight there after a long, hard day. Nearby is a beaver pond that is definitely occupied.

In the morning, trail friend Chuck Anderson met me at US 20 and drove me to Lee, Massachusetts, and back. He bought me breakfast when I really needed a boost. The October Mountain Lean-to must taste good to porcupines. In '48 they were much more numerous—practically a plague.

The Trail goes through Dalton, Massachusetts, past the home of Tom Levardi, who had a sign in front of his house advertising water. He invited me in for pie and ice cream. This region of small towns and hospitable people can slow the progress of hikers. If all of the Trail were like this, a thru-hike would be almost impossible because of the lure to spend time with these friendly folks.

I slept near the Crystal Mountain Campsite, then continued on to The Cobbles. This vista provides a fine view of the town of Cheshire, known for its "Big Cheese," and for Elder John Leland, father of religious liberty in America.

Mount Greylock—at 3,487 feet the highest point in Massachusetts—has a road to the top, a lodge, and a war memorial. I stopped to sleep near Notch Road. Then I side-trailed to Williamstown, Massachusetts, and a store. The regular bridge across the Hoosic River was closed for repairs, but fortunately another bridge provided a detour. Beyond the bridge, the Trail suddenly turned up a driveway. A man there provided water and the usual talk session. From there the Trail follows Sherman Brook, then ascends gradually to the Massachusetts/Vermont state line.

A brook in Sages Ravine, Mount Washington State Park, Connecticut

A squirrel peeks out from its nest above the Trail

A very unusual insect, this walking stick was found on a trail sign

♦♦♦

A pair of ringnecked pheasants combing through fallen leaves

A swallowtail butterfly on a lilac bush

◆ ◆ ◆

Loons are part of the varied bird life found along the Trail

Rock lichens create colorful layered patterns

Next page: *Moonrise over the ruins of a stone tower atop Bear Mountain in Connecticut*

Mountain Moon Sonnet

Tagg Run leaps down along its boulder course,
Singing a soft sonata as it goes
Through bordered aisles of sapling growth and gorse
Scented with nepenthe and sweet aloes.

Soft moonlight trickles through the canopy
Of fledgling leaves to dance upon the stream
In twinkling silver fire and dulcet glee
With all the winsome madness of a dream.

O, hush-strewn night upon the mountainside,
Replete with moonlight-spangled stream and trees,
Can beauty so compelling be denied?
Is there aught else that could ignoble these?

Massachusetts/Vermont border
to the Connecticut River

Past the Vermont state line the Appalachian Trail coincides with the Long Trail, the country's first long-distance trail, which extends from there all the way to Canada. The Appalachian Trail overlaps it for a hundred miles before turning eastward toward the White Mountains. This terrain was familiar to me, as very little relocating has been done.

A college orientation group crowded the new Seth Warner Shelter and Primitive Camping Area, so I went on about a mile before stopping for the night. This preemption by institutional organizations is a problem for thru-hikers, especially in Vermont. A heavy thunderstorm during the night didn't help matters any.

Harmon Hill overlooks the historic town of Bennington, Vermont. A Scout group staying at Melville Nauheim Shelter gave me supper and a place to stay in the shelter—very welcome.

During the day, the weather got so nasty that I stopped and huddled under a poncho for a while, then continued on to Goddard Shelter for the night.

On Stratton Mountain I paused to recall that Benton MacKaye was in the top of a tree on this mountain when the idea for the Appalachian Trail came to him. A plaque has been placed there. Mr. MacKaye had graduated from Dartmouth College in 1900 and

A piece of fallen birch bark, Baker Peak, Vermont

then hiked the length of the Green Mountains with a friend. He went to work for the U.S. Forest Service as a regional planner, setting up national forests and parks. He told me he had personally scouted some of them. I visited and had long discussions with him after my hike in '48.

The Appalachian Trail is the dream come true of Mr. MacKaye. In 1921 he wrote an article for the journal of the American Institute of Architects titled "An Appalachian Trail: A Project in Regional Planning." Among my personal treasures is an original reprint of this article, inscribed at the top of the page with these words from Mr. MacKaye: "To Earl Shaffer, of the A.T., a man who did it from one who wrote it. Benton MacKaye."

A side trail now goes to the gondola station on Stratton Mountain, with free rides to thru-hikers to the ski center below, where an all-you-can-eat buffet is available. Some of those who were there ate so much they almost exploded!

At Stratton Pond I went astray, following the old, familiar Trail to the far side before realizing that Stratton View Shelter had been removed and the Trail relocated on the other side of the pond. The point of wrong-turning had no proper marking. After a few hundred yards the other way, I finally spotted a blaze. The traditional method of marking,

Opposite: *The view west from Baker Peak in Vermont*

A stream plunges down White Cliff Mountain in Vermont

which allowed you to see a blaze on the front and back of the same tree, was replaced with staggered blazes on different trees because some said the old markings detracted from the wilderness feel.

Many of the shelters in Vermont have been either renamed or replaced since '48. One of the shelters no longer in existence was named for John Vondell, an Amherst College professor and a key leader and worker on the New England portion of the Trail. I met and talked with him in '48 when he was on a work trip.

At sunset I stopped and slept about 2 miles from the pond. Beyond that is the intersection with the side trail leading to the William B. Douglas Shelter. Despite common belief, the shelter was not named in honor of the late Chief Justice of the U.S. Supreme Court, William O. Douglas, who was the 18th thru-hiker of the Appalachian Trail.

I hitchhiked to Manchester Center, Vermont, to a grocery store, laundromat, and restaurant—always the targets of thru-hikers in town. Back on the Trail, I came to the ski resort at Bromley Mountain. The lodge is still there, but the "dancing stove" I remembered from my Long Cruise is gone. In '48 I met two young men along the Trail who were staying at the Bromley Lodge, where we had an eventful dinner together. Here's how I described the scene in my book, *Walking With Spring*:

> The way those college fellers started a fire was a sight to behold, from a distance. First pour some gasoline from a bottle into a dish, dump it into the chunk stove, and back off while lighting a match. The result was a ball of fire, a roar, and a dancing stove. After recovering my power of speech I told them they wouldn't start many fires that way. The food they produced would have fed a small army; then out came the dishtowels, Brillo pads, scouring powder, and various other aids to successful housekeeping. No wonder they needed two trips to carry out their gear.

It's a wonder that those college boys didn't set the place on fire by using gasoline!

The Appalachian Trail along Baker Peak in Vermont

101

"At times I had been finding notes attached to trees, from a reporter who said he was anxious to meet me. I resolved to avoid him if possible, but it was in vain."

I stopped hiking early to spend the night at Big Branch Shelter. Farther on at Little Rock Pond, one of my favorite old shelters had been removed—too much use and abuse. The shelter, situated on an island, was too nice and too near a road. A new shelter and tenting area have been built beyond the pond, with a caretaker on duty.

A high suspension bridge now spans Clarendon Gorge. In '48 it was scramble through any old way. I went to Clarendon Shelter and slept a mile beyond that.

The next day I passed the Killington and Pico Peak ski areas. By evening I was at Sherburne Pass and slept nearby. A relocation has placed the turnoff toward the White Mountains beyond a lodge I remembered from '48. I missed the turn at this point and had to retrace my steps about a mile.

In '48 this section toward New Hampshire was dubbed "the missing link." It hadn't been maintained for a decade and was badly overgrown. That was the only time on the Long Cruise when my compass came in handy. This section has been relocated over mountains instead of through valleys, making it much more difficult. I covered only about 9 miles before stopping at Stony Brook Shelter. Some of this section is as tough as it can be, especially the needless crossing of a pinnacle.

My stopping point the next night was beyond Wintturi Shelter. The day had been rainy and it continued through the night—an unhappy one.

At West Hartford, Vermont, the Trail passes a country store, where I met "Yogi" and "Boo Boo" for the first time in two months. The ice cream—blackberry—was the best I'd ever eaten. The

A marsh north of Blue Hill Road in Massachusetts

boots Boo Boo was wearing were in tatters and he was waiting for new ones to arrive. That night I slept at Happy Hill Shelter.

At times I had been finding notes attached to trees, from a reporter who said he was anxious to meet me. I resolved to avoid him if possible, but it was in vain. Near Norwich, Vermont, he came to meet me and walked along with me. He proved to be the friendliest and most obliging reporter met on the trip. He drove me to a store to get a down vest, which was sorely needed—and even bought me lunch. On second thought, Bill Bowden from the *York Daily Record* had been just as accommodating.

◆ ◆ ◆

Reflections in Griffith Lake, Vermont

Next page: *Appalachian Trail fence stile near Beacon Hill, Vermont*

The Trail goes through an old tree plantation near Bunker Hill, Vermont

Evergreen

From tropic swamp to polar snows,
From tidal shore to timberline,
Wherever vegetation grows,
The greatest constancy is mine.

Your eyes will tire of colors new,
Though seasonal or changing scene,
And turn away from every hue
But rest with ease on evergreen.

Connecticut River *to the* New Hampshire/Maine border

After crossing the Connecticut River and passing through Hanover, New Hampshire, I stopped for the night near Moose Mountain Shelter, where a Dartmouth orientation group was in residence. The next day a touch of autumn was in the air and that ominous wind song was in the treetops. The down vest came just in time!

At Holts Ledge, the Trail skirts a deep, wide valley but bypasses the cabin where I stayed in '48. Lots of people were out for the day. Some of them stopped me to give me snacks, and one took me to a store and back. I slept south of the Firewarden's Cabin on Smarts Mountain.

After crossing Mount Mist to Glencliff, New Hampshire, I was invited to stay at the home of Henry and Carla Lafleur. The Lafleurs offered me various items of clothing, including a stocking cap to replace the one I had lost. They are truly trail angels.

Mount Moosilauke is the first above-timberline peak the northbound hiker crosses on the Trail, and by far the highest mountain encountered since Apple Orchard Mountain in central Virginia. The climb from Glencliff is about 5 or 6 steady miles. It is difficult to believe that a stage road once went to the summit, where a lodge was located until it was struck by lightning and burned. The old shelter next to the summit was removed and the small spring nearby is not dependable.

A maple sapling on a birch root, Crawford Notch, New Hampshire

On a clear day, the Presidentials, especially Mount Washington, are highly visible. From here on, much of the Appalachian Trail is near or above timberline and has some of the worst weather on earth. The area lies between the warm Gulf Stream in the Atlantic and the Arctic areas of Canada. Changes can be sudden and deadly, so it's good to be prepared.

After the rock ramble across Mount Moosilauke's long summit comes a steep descent on Beaver Brook Trail, which actually is a rock climb in reverse. Close beside it is the brook, a series of swirling waterfalls. Light rain was falling on Beaver Brook Trail, increasing as I crossed Kinsman Notch and started traversing Kinsman Ridge. At twilight I was about halfway to Eliza Brook Shelter and had to stop and sleep as best I could.

The rain continued in the morning. I arrived at Eliza Brook Shelter in the afternoon. The shelter was full but not crowded, so I was able to stay. Several tents were set up nearby. Tim, who had been hiking a few days ahead of me in Virginia, was at the shelter. He said he had injured his foot and had to stop until it healed. He's a fast and capable hiker, and he resumed the trip early in the morning. I didn't see him again.

Opposite: *A footbridge leads the way to Velvet Rocks, New Hampshire*

The Appalachian Trail, Mount Moriah, New Hampshire

Hawk Migration

Lesser cousins of the eagles
But they soar with equal ease
And ride the upward windstream
Where it skims the crestline trees.

Things were getting rough, especially the weather. Wondered if I would be able to struggle on. As I left the shelter later, someone remarked, "I hope you like water." The brook I had to wade was knee-deep. I didn't like it. It didn't really matter: My boots were already soggy. The rain eased later near Lonesome Lake Hut, the first of the Appalachian Mountain Club's high-level hostels that northbound hikers encounter in the White Mountains. The hut keeper gave me a soggy cinnamon bun he had baked.

At Franconia Notch, Betty and Bill Robinson, owners of the Cascade Lodge B & B in North Woodstock, New Hampshire, met me and invited me for an overnight stay and a restaurant meal. In the morning they shuttled me back to the notch. Resting there was "The Family," consisting of a mother and her five children, ranging in age from eight to twenty-two. I wondered whether they would be able to complete their thru-hike under the increasingly difficult conditions.

A local park workman came along in a truck and drove me to a country store and back. He also gave me an old down-filled parka, which would come in mighty handy later.

The climb up Liberty Mountain is steep and rocky and the ridge-crest to Mount Lafayette is narrow and difficult. In '48 the Trail didn't go here. Now it threads the multi-topped Lafayette, where you look ahead and think the Trail can't go there. But it does. As I left the peak, the sun was sinking. Luckily I found a spot among the stunted spruce that was clear and level enough to lie down on.

The next day I went astray on a high point, downhill for several miles. Hikers who were coming up from the valley convinced me to

Swirling water of Beaver Brook on Blue Mountain, New Hampshire

109

turn back. This lost me almost half a day. At Galehead Hut the crew said I should have called for a reservation but then decided to let me stay anyway. Call from where?

The night was foggy and rainy, but the sky cleared the next day at Zealand Falls. I stopped to talk to some people before continuing on to the shelter at Ethan Pond for the night.

At Crawford Notch I hitchhiked to a store and back, waded the Saco River, climbed Webster Cliffs, then crossed Mount Webster and Mount Jackson to Mizpah Hut before stopping there for the night. This is a deluxe structure replacing the small pole shelter at the site in '48. One of the hut crew members had a guitar and we played and sang. To my amazement, the younger people were fascinated by the genuine folk songs I sang that they had never heard before—songs that everyone had sung 60 years ago in school and at home. I have a notebook containing 300 titles, and the list isn't complete.

A storm blew by in the night and the day dawned cold and windy. Ravens were swooping around in the wind. At Lakes of the Clouds Hut, about a dozen hikers were resting and eating and debating what to do. That hut was closed for the season, and so was Madison Springs Hut, the next shelter north. Between them are about 7 miles of nothing but rocks. A crosswind that must have been gusting about 100 miles an hour was making things miserable on Mount Washington, the highest peak in New England at 6,288 feet elevation. A weather station on the top of the mountain has recorded the strongest surface wind velocity ever, anywhere, at 231 miles per hour.

We decided to take the bypass from the summit of Mount Washington down Tuckerman Ravine to Pinkham Notch Camp. With the violent weather and the bad reputation of the Whites, it would be foolish to risk continuing. I was soon wondering about our decision because the ravine is steep and crumbly, but we all got down safely.

"The next day a touch of autumn was in the air and that ominous wind song was in the treetops. The down vest came just in time!"

Bruce Pettingill of "Hiker's Paradise" in Gorham, New Hampshire, was shuttling hikers. He persuaded me to go along with him, so I did —and didn't regret it. In the morning he drove me to a store before shuttling me back to Pinkham Notch. The other hikers who were there said they were taking a break. Never saw them again.

Some time or other I had twisted my knee and it was stiffening in the cold. My progress was slow for the 6 miles to Carter Notch Hut. As I left to make the steep climb from Carter Notch Hut, there wasn't a cloud in the sky. Looking back, I saw a puff of smoke from the cog railway on Mount Washington. Down the far slope of Carter Dome was enough for another short day, and I slept that night on a mossy spot near Imp Campsite.

In the morning I crossed Mount Moriah and passed Rattle River Shelter to US 2, where trail angel Earle Towne of "The Cabin" in Andover, Maine, shuttled me back to Gorham to a store. Then I continued on Cascade Mountain and slept by the Trail. At last the White Mountains were behind me!

Extra loops of the Appalachian Mountain Club trail system have been added, making the Trail even tougher than it was before. And what of Maine? I'd been warned that the Trail has changed greatly and is much more difficult. Plus October was closing in, and Mount Katahdin is often snowbound by then.

The New Hampshire/Maine state line was 10 miles away. I passed Dream Lake, Gentian Pond, and Mount Success—all well-remembered from 50 years ago. In the morning I saw a flock of crows, or ravens. The main difference is in size. A hawk or an eagle also flew by.

I slept somewhere near the Maine state line, the last state border crossing on the Trail for the northbound traveler.

The Appalachian Trail heads toward Lake of the Clouds, New Hampshire

Next page: *Star Lake and distant Mount Washington,*
        White Mountain National Forest, New Hampshire

Mountaineer Manifesto

You can go back to your city,
Back to your factories and mills
Where everything's smoky and gritty,
But I'll go back to my hills.

You can go back to your fancy home,
Back to your tailored togs;
I'll go back where the wild deer roam,
Back to my cabin of logs.

You can go back to your swimming pool,
Back to your troublesome bills;
I'll swim again in a streamlet cool,
Back in my peaceful hills.

The evenings you'll spend on a dance floor
I'll spend out under the stars,
And find in my solitude once more
A balm for my wounds and scars.

I'll purge all my hatred, or try to,
Live as a free man again.
Do as I like when I want to,
Go where I choose to and when.

No offered position could lure me,
No chance for gain or renown
Could ever beguile or detour me
To coop myself up in a town.

You may take wide spacious highways
To offices, factories, and mills,
But I'll take the trails and the byways
That lead to my peaceful hills.

New Hampshire/Maine border *to* Mount Katahdin

Ahead of me were almost 300 miles to the end of the Trail, most of it rerouted since '48. Rumor has it that the Trail through Maine is longer and rougher than any other section, with steep rock climbs, high stone steps, and bogs crossed on single-log "bridges."

Mount Carlo and Goose Eye Mountain are treeless on top but have stunted growth among the rocks. Then comes the most incredible and difficult mile on the Appalachian Trail— Mahoosuc Notch. You crawl and scramble through a deep cleft, over and under giant boulders. Underneath is ice that has been there almost forever. One man said he took his dog through in three hours. It took me longer than that.

Rain was threatening as I emerged at the north end of the notch and climbed Old Speck, the third-highest peak in Maine. It is obviously a long-extinct volcano, with its deep lake in the center. The shelter is next to the pond. Several hikers were already there. The weather blew clear and cold during the night.

When I set out the next day, a strong wind was crossing the crater's west rim. My fingers got frostbitten in spite of my wearing wool socks over them. I was hungry and weak, having run out of food the day before. The Trail had been relocated on the north side of Old Speck and I was about to follow the old route until I realized that if something should happen, no one would be looking for me there.

At Grafton Notch I finally got a ride with a state park ranger to the town of Bethel, Maine—and to a store, for much-needed food supplies. There, trail angels "Honey" and "Bear" (Margie and Earle Towne) offered me an overnight stay at The Cabin in Andover, Maine. We had a singing session in the evening.

In the morning, Earle shuttled me back to Grafton Notch. The car window was iced over, but the wind had died. Birch leaves were turning orange, in pleasing contrast with the evergreens. Even at high levels there is vegetation. Small tundra-type plants, tiny but brilliant, flourish between the rocks.

The face of Baldpate Mountain should be posted "For rock climbers only." In '48 the Trail did not include this slanting, almost smooth rock face. It followed the tree line to the right. Past Baldpate, the Frye Notch Lean-to is an old one, probably built by Louis Chorzempa, who spent several summers building lean-tos in Maine.

At Dunn Notch a beautiful waterfall drops sheer into a rock grotto. Beyond is a long escarpment, dropping steeply to the right to East B Hill Road. Earle Towne was waiting there to shuttle hikers back to

Maple trees on Little Boardman Mountain, Maine

The Cabin. From there I called John, who said he was glad to hear from me and that I was moving on. Bruce from Hiker's Paradise in Gorham, New Hampshire, had called him, explaining that I was discouraged and had talked about quitting, and that John had better come and get me. But with encouragement from Margie and Earle, my mood changed. Their message was, "Carry on, Ridgerunner. You can't quit now, with only a few hundred miles to go."

So I hiked on to Wyman Mountain before stopping at sunset to sleep under tall evergreens. On this section you wade Sawyer Brook, struggle over the long crossing of Moody Mountain, and then have to wade Black Brook at South Arm Road. Earle was on duty and I couldn't turn down another chance to stay at The Cabin and eat Margie's cooking.

My progress had slowed, but at least I didn't quit. Old Blue Mountain, not on the Trail in '48, is a really tough ascent. It's what is sometimes described as "hand and foot" or "hand over hand."

On Bemis Mountain I was caught in a sudden violent thunder-storm and was forced to stop. The terrain was so rough that the only place to sleep was on the Trail, and that was rocky. It seemed as though the night would never end. In '65, Bemis Mountain was one of my best stops. On that trip I awoke to see a giant white-tail buck standing like a statue before disappearing, but this time it was where I spent the most miserable night so far.

Thoroughly soaked, I crossed the long summit through the wet woods—another day of rocks and roots and mudholes—then stopped to dry out and recuperate. I went only as far as ME 17 before hitching another shuttle to The Cabin, which was becoming a habit for me. Dave Donaldson, "Spirit of '48," was there. In the morning Dave and I hiked on together, deciding to team up for the rest of the hike. Maine in late autumn is not a place to hike alone.

The next day we managed to reach ME 4—and another shuttle to The Cabin. What would I have done without Honey and Bear?

In the morning Dave and I passed Piazza Rock Lean-to and then started over Saddleback Mountain, skirting the ski area below. An overcast sky limited the view, which extends into Canada. Between Saddleback and Saddleback Junior is The Horn, several miles of high

The Appalachian Trail heading north along Bemis Mountain

trail. Except for Mount Katahdin, this is the mountain showplace of Maine. The cold and windy weather continued to Poplar Ridge Lean-to.

Dave and I made our way to Orbeton Stream and across Spaulding Mountain. Along the way we saw a spruce grouse hen and heard geese calling. The weather at Spaulding Mountain Lean-to remained cold, with rain and wind.

In the morning I awoke, looked out at the rain-and-wind-wracked woods, and said to Dave, "I can't. I can't. I'll wait here until the weather clears, then head for home." Yet at the same time I was pulling on my wet, cold boots onto my shivering feet and getting my pack ready to move on, muttering to myself, "You've known all along that this is your last hike. Isn't that why you couldn't stay home? Make the most of it. The cracked rib is healed, the twisted knee is better, the black eye and bruises are gone. The stress and strain, the rocks and roots and deep mudholes, the logs over bogs, the sheer rock climbs, and cold rivers to wade are part of the package, so carry on." Dave looked puzzled but said nothing.

The rain was lessening at the side trail to Sugarloaf Mountain, the second highest peak in Maine. Sugarloaf was on the Trail in '48 but has since been turned into a ski resort. A hurricane in 1938 had wrecked this section of the Trail and it was officially closed for many years. Dave and I crossed Carrabassett River, mostly on rocks, and arrived at Caribou Valley Road, where Earle Towne picked us up to shuttle us back to The Cabin. He and Margie certainly were doing all they could to help me on my way.

After 9 miles crossing North and South Crocker Mountains, we camped at Cranberry Stream Campsite. I had been warned months ago that 9 or 10 miles was a good daily average in Maine these days. It's true.

We came to the Bigelow Range, where new lean-tos have been built. The range bears the name of a colonel who accompanied Benedict Arnold on his ill-fated expedition to Canada. At the other end of the ridge is Avery Peak, named for Captain Myron H. Avery, former longtime Appalachian Trail Conference chairman. We stopped at the Avery Memorial Campsite at Bigelow Col. In the northeast, the term "col" refers to a deep gap between two high

A spruce grouse on Bemis Mountain

◆ ◆ ◆

A bull moose peers through the trees on Sugarloaf Mountain

A beaver pond along Holly Brook

◆ ◆ ◆

Earl Shaffer in front of Moxie Bald Shelter

points in a mountain range. The ominous weather threatened a blizzard, which did not come. In good weather, Katahdin is visible from Little Bigelow, which rises beyond Bigelow Col.

Little Bigelow is on the far side on the way down to East Flagstaff Road, where we met my brother John. He had come to Maine to make final arrangements for an interview with Harry Smith of CBS.

Dave and I then hiked on past West Carry Pond and met Harry Smith and the CBS crew at a logging road, where they followed along with us for two days to the Kennebec River.

We crossed the Kennebec River by canoe, courtesy of Steve Longley of Rivers and Trails, who operates the ferry service. Earle Towne was at the river with a group of hikers, and they presented me with a bright blue jacket, shirt, and cap, suitably inscribed. The jacket would look good on a high school athlete. At night it was raining hard, so Dave and I slept in John's van.

John and Dave and I had a decision to make. John had been in touch with Baxter State Park Superintendent Irving "Buzz" Caverly, who said that Katahdin had been closed for a week because of ice on rocks, but the weather had moderated and a climb the next day might be possible. It might be the last chance to climb before next summer. Most of the thru-hikers were in the same predicament. We decided to shuttle to the mountain and climb it, then return to fill in the gap. Others did the same.

If the Trail in Maine had remained as described in Myron Avery's *Silver Aisle*, we would have reached Katahdin in September. You appreciate the difficulty of the current Trail when you read the sign at the edge of the "100-Mile Wilderness" that says, "Don't enter this area without a 10-day supply of food." The original route passed sporting camps and went through towns that are now bypassed, so today's hikers must either make side trips to those same towns or arrange for food to be delivered, as John did for us. John was staying in Maine to help us finish the Trail. Without him we probably would have failed.

We were joined at Katahdin Stream Campground by about two dozen other thru-hikers who had been awaiting a chance to climb.

(I'll save the description of this final climb until the end of this account.) After Katahdin we hiked from Abol Bridge at the Penobscot River back to the base of the mountain, completing the portion of the Trail through Baxter State Park, which was about to close for the season.

Afterward we returned to the Kennebec River to hike the remaining 150 miles north to Abol Bridge. Dave and I reached Moxie Bald Lean-to. After an early start and a long, rainy day of hiking, we were shuttled to Shaw's Boarding Home in Monson, Maine—the last Trail town for northbounders—for a good supper and sleep. Then, after an even better breakfast, we were shuttled back to the Trail.

The section north of Moxie Pond has many stream wadings and the levels were high because of the steady rain. After about 14 sloggy miles, we shuttled again to Shaw's Boarding Home. Proprietors Keith and Pat Shaw said, "You're lucky; we have steak tonight." I'll say. Breakfast was fried potatoes, pancakes, sausage, and eggs. Then we had another long, hard day, crossing ME 15 to enter the 100-Mile Wilderness. We slept near Little Wilson Falls. In the morning we waded the boulder-bottomed Big Wilson Stream and finally reached Long Pond Stream Lean-to, where someone had left sausage and cheese, which we consumed gratefully.

Maine in October can be described as rocks, roots, seldom sunshine, frosted fingers, fog, and rain. We crossed Chairback Mountain to the lean-to, which was crowded with thru-hikers, but they made room for us.

In the morning, thru-hiker "Alice in Wonderland" came crying and shaking, half-dead from exposure. Always the gentleman, Dave handed her the breakfast he had just finished cooking. She had spent the cold, rainy night with her back against a tree a mile short of the shelter. John was waiting at the next logging road and he took "Alice" to the Appalachian Trail Lodge in Millinocket, Maine. The lodge owner also has a restaurant down the street, where about two dozen thru-hikers had congregated. The cooks and waitresses were very busy!

A pond in the 100-Mile Wilderness

The eastern peak of Baldpate Mountain in the Mahoosuc Range

Back on the Trail, we forded the West Branch of Pleasant River and were about to move on when a crowd of school kids came swarming through the water. They turned off on the Gulf Hagas Trail. Gulf Hagas, called "The Grand Canyon of the East," is a fantastically beautiful, deep, and narrow gorge with many waterfalls.

From here the relocated Trail crosses three additional peaks, none of them with good views. The only redeeming feature is a campsite honoring Sidney Tappan, a fine gentleman who spent a lot of time working on the Trail in Maine. We were both on a work trip at Long Pond, and he and I visited Gulf Hagas together.

By the time we had crossed those three summits, the sun was setting, but we climbed White Cap Mountain. White Cap is near timberline, with stunted trees. We finally had to sleep on the Trail itself because of the dense undergrowth. For the first time we had an open view of Katahdin, beyond the Lake Country of central Maine.

It must have been Indian Summer, as the weather had turned sunny and warm. Descending from White Cap we passed East Branch Lean-to, waded across the East Branch of Pleasant River, passed Little Boardman Mountain, and stopped at Cooper Brook Falls Lean-to. The nearby stream is so noisy that we had difficulty sleeping.

Next we passed Antlers Campsite, where a sporting camp had been operating in '48, and Lower Jo-Mary Lake, named for a famous Indian guide. Later we stopped to drink at Potaywadjo Spring, one of the finest springs along the entire Appalachian Trail, and made our way to Nahmakanta Stream Campsite for the night.

Atop Mount Katahdin in Baxter State Park

The next day we passed Nahmakanta Lake. We stopped for the night at Rainbow Stream Lean-to. Reporters joined us there in the morning and walked along with us over Rainbow Ledges to Hurd Brook Lean-to, where admirers, photographers, more reporters, and three TV taping crews joined the procession.

The thru-hike actually ended at Abol Bridge because we had previously hiked from that point to the base of Katahdin. Here begins the account of our Katahdin climb.

As mentioned before, about two dozen thru-hikers had been waiting for a chance to climb Katahdin, and they joined us at Katahdin Stream Campground. The weather was wonderful. My nephew Bob, who had been with me at the beginning of this trip, came in from Seattle to be there at the end. Trail friends Gail and Dan Johnson had driven up from South Carolina. Gail, or "Gutsy," who also had met me at the beginning of this trip, was a seasoned thru-hiker, but Dan would be climbing Katahdin for the first time. Also joining us was a filmmaker named Huey from Portland, Maine. He and his crew were filming for a documentary on Katahdin.

The Hunt Spur, the route the Trail follows up Katahdin, is like a boulder ridge turned vertically, a jumbled mass. You look up and say, "This can't be a trail." But you scramble and heave and up you go. As in '48, I was carrying my pack. It wouldn't be fair to leave it behind.

Then, suddenly, the rock climbing ends at the "Gateway"— two stones set on end. Beyond is the last mile north on the Trail, stretching across a rocky tableland to the rock cairn and sign on Baxter Peak. Midway is Thoreau Spring, named after its discoverer, Henry David Thoreau.

Earl Shaffer on top of Mount Katahdin in 1948

◆◆◆

Earl completes his 1998 Anniversary Hike on Mount Katahdin

Baxter Peak bears the name of Percival Baxter, the former Maine governor who personally bought and donated the vast area encircling Mount Katahdin for use as a state park. It took him 30 years. His vision and generosity have preserved this "King of Mountains" from the commercial exploitation and encroachment of civilization that have mutilated so many outstanding peaks including Mount Washington, Clingmans Dome, and Mount Mitchell. He specified that Katahdin remain primitive. It is one of the most beautiful mountains on earth to look at—and to look *from*.

I have climbed Katahdin eight times and stayed on the top overnight when that was still allowed. The first time, the sky was full of Northern Lights. The second time was in the midst of a driving rain.

This time the hikers—most of them thru-hikers—clustered around the sign, talking and taking pictures, lingering as though reluctant to end their odyssey. We had to be down before nightfall. Ranger "Buzz" treated us to a banquet dinner and allowed us to sleep in the guesthouse.

In the still of the night, a poem came from out of somewhere to scribble and keep
To honor a mountain of noble name that reaches for sunrise from valleys deep:

Katahdin

You love it and you fear it,
It is wild and harsh and high,
A mass of ancient granite
Towering into the sky.
For Indians who revered it
And the climbers of today,
A symbol of a spirit
That will never pass away.

Opposite: *Mount Katahdin reflected in the West Branch of the Penebscot River*

AFTERWORD
The Best Birthday Present Of Them All

by Linda Ellerbee

I wonder what the old man's doing for Thanksgiving dinner. Eating turkey with plenty of mashed potatoes and gravy, I hope. When I saw him, Fig Newtons figured large in his diet. But that was back in August, along the Appalachian Trail, on a mountain near the Massachusetts/Connecticut border. I thought it surprising *I* was there—until I met the old man.

It was the third day of my 40-mile hike. I was celebrating my 54th birthday. Each year I walk a little farther, always alone. So far, time on the trail had been hot, hard, and wonderful, but getting to the top of this particular mountain was rough. Now I was heading down, sympathizing with my knees (going downhill, your knees hurt; uphill, everything else does).

I rounded another bend in the trail, and there came this old man. He looked like anything but today's backpacker (who's usually outfitted in clothes composed entirely of chemicals and carrying a pack large enough to house a family, filled with pounds of high-tech gear, including the latest "necessary" gadget—the hiker's espresso machine).

The old man carried a small canvas rucksack, the kind kids use to carry their schoolbooks. He wore faded pants, a flannel shirt, and a pith helmet with mosquito netting. Assuming him to be either the

A cascade above Zealand Falls, New Hampshire

world's most determined panhandler or an unshaven, elderly gentleman out for a hard day's hike, I asked where he'd started.

"Georgia."

I gasped. The Appalachian Trail is a footpath that begins at Springer Mountain in Georgia, and ends at Mount Katahdin in Maine. In between are roughly 2,160 miles and more than 400 mountains big enough to have names. Those who thru-hike (walk it end to end in one big bite) usually start in early spring and finish in September or October. Each year some 1,500 start, about 300 finish.

Like old age itself, the Appalachian Trail is not for sissies. The first man to thru-hike it was a Pennsylvanian named Earl Shaffer, back in 1948. Mr. Shaffer was 29 and, judging from his photographs, in great shape, but in his report to the Appalachian Trail Conference, he said that words failed to describe the hardships: "Gradually the trail became a seemingly endless venture, so that I was probably the most amazed of all when I finally reached trail's end. I often pondered whether the difficulties provided me with the impetus to carry me along."

Sometimes, on my hikes, I thought of Earl Shaffer's words, both in the context of literal hills and in the broader context of my life. Instead of obstacles being merely things to overcome, was it, in fact,

Cheshire viewed from The Cobbles Overlook in Massachusetts

the hard stuff that kept me going? Is there something about struggle that is necessary for survival?

The old man in my path was, unbelievably, three quarters of the way to Maine. I asked, politely, exactly how old he was. He said 79. I asked if he was having a good time. He said no. (His eyes said he might be lying about that.) I asked why he didn't quit. He said because he'd started, that's why. I asked why he'd started. He said it was the 50th anniversary of the first time he'd done it.

"No kidding? You made this trek 50 years ago? Why, that would be in, uh, 1948, right?" He nodded.

"Wow. Then you must have known…" I stopped and stood very still, thinking. No way. Couldn't be. "Uh, sir…what is your name?"

"Earl."

"I see. And would your last name be, by any chance, Shaffer?"

He admitted it was. Stunned, I told him that months ago I'd read that Earl Shaffer was planning to try hiking the length of the trail again this year, but I had thought this was, well, hype. I mean, 79 years old?

Two thousand miles of mountains? I said running into him was the best birthday present of all. He smiled and walked on. Toward Maine. Toward tomorrow.

And I thought: He may claim he did it to celebrate an anniversary, but I think Mr. Shaffer knew what he was talking about when he said life's difficulties gave him the wherewithal to carry on. Lord knows he was carrying on. Then I had another thought. I turned and called out, "What's been the worst part of the hike this time?"

Earl Shaffer answered without looking back: "Reporters and their questions."

And so it goes.

Reprinted with permission from Linda Ellerbee, 2001.

This article was first published in the November 1998 issue of New Choices. *Linda Ellerbee is a former NBC correspondent and best-selling author who now runs her own award-winning TV production company, Lucky Duck.*

THE APPALACHIAN TRAIL CONFERENCE

Since its founding in 1925 by private citizens and early leaders of the new national forests and parks in the eastern United States, the Appalachian Trail Conference (ATC) has operated under several guiding principles. According to the ATC's constitution, the first principle has been to "promote, construct and manage…a connected trail, with related trails, to be called the Appalachian Trail and to preserve and restore the natural environment of the Trail and its adjacent lands"—the lands photographer Bart Smith has captured in the images that fill this book. "This Trail shall run, as far as practicable, over the summits of the mountains and through the wild lands of the Atlantic Seaboard and adjoining states from Maine to Georgia, so as to render accessible for hiking, backpacking and other forms of primitive travel and living, the said mountains and woodlands."

The second principle has been to protect that footpath from the creep of development—a commitment that began in 1935 as the idea of a wilderness corridor started to take shape, and has been at the forefront of the efforts on behalf of the Trail ever since. In 1968 those efforts led to the passage of the National Trails System Act, designating "the A.T." a National Scenic Trail and authorizing acquisition with public funds of a small buffer of land around it. The last of the hundreds of parcels that make up that buffer—the most complicated public-land protection program in federal history—is expected to be purchased in 2002. But the ATC, which still centers on local volunteers and their public-agency land-management partners, nonetheless invests significant resources in monitoring and rebuffing encroachments on the nation's longest, skinniest unit of the National Park System, one of the country's few "natural resource parks."

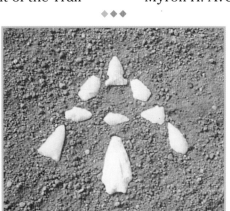

AT symbol made from arrowheads collected by Earl Shaffer in 1948

❖❖❖

When those principles were adopted during the early years of the A.T., the only thought given to a one-season hike of the entire Trail, then about 2,000 miles long, was to dismiss the possibility entirely. Benton MacKaye, the founder of the ATC and first proponent of the Trail, saw it as a refuge from metropolitan degradation of the human spirit, and as a means to study nature. ATC leader Captain Myron H. Avery organized the volunteer clubs and led the 200-odd volunteers who actually built and shaped the A.T. into an existing continuous footpath. He saw the A.T. as a means to stay physically fit, recreation within a pleasing natural environment.

In 1948 a 29-year-old World War II veteran just back from the South Pacific, seeking relief from the war's sadness in nature's own poetry, set out to walk end-to-end this trail he had read about. In being the first that August to report such a continuous walk—and prove it to the satisfaction of a skeptical Captain Avery and Jean Stephenson, editor of the *Appalachian Trailway News*—Earl V. Shaffer defined the term "thru-hike" and gave the Appalachian Trail a whole new dimension that captured the public's imagination from that point onward.

And, it can be argued that Earl Shaffer gave the ATC yet another guiding principle: active engagement with, and advice for, those who would explore its treasures, large and small. Since the 1930s the ATC had published guidebooks, maps, and brochures, but Earl brought home the day-to-day aspects of long-distance hiking on the A.T. For about five years following his 1948 hike, he served as the ATC's corresponding secretary, answering the mail from would-be end-to-enders, showing his slides (still a staple of the recovering thru-hiker), and telling his stories.

His single, typed page of advice garnered on his 1948 hike—including a pack weight of 20 pounds plus food, and such gems as "diet can be varied by immediate consumption when visiting stores"—is a classic among today's guidebooks on hiking the A.T. "Good planning, a sturdy physique, exceptional determination, and ingenious adaptability are essential on a long and strenuous foot journey.... Above all, do not underestimate the difficulties involved or overestimate your own capabilities. Both good luck and good management are necessary," he wrote then.

Moreover, he built shelters, helped found the Susquehanna Appalachian Trail Club and the Keystone Trails Association (a group of local Trail-maintainers), and furthered political efforts to bring the footpath under federal protection. He went on in 1965 to hike end-to-end again, this time beginning in Maine, becoming the first person known to have hiked the A.T. in both directions.

Later, in the 1980s, he donated to the ATC a more tangible legacy: the proceeds from his previously self-published book *Walking With Spring*, in which he chronicled his first thru-hike.

As the ATC has become a model for volunteer-centered public and private cooperative management of public recreational lands, Earl Shaffer has become not only an inspiration for the thousands of thru-hikers who followed, but also a model for giving back to the Appalachian Trail project.

—Brian King

Brian King has served as director of public affairs for the Appalachian Trail Conference since 1987. For more information about the Appalachian Trail Conference, call 1-888-287-8673; visit the website at www.appalachiantrail.org; or write to ATC, P.O. Box 807, Harpers Ferry, WV 25425.

A lone tree atop Silers Bald, Nantahala National Forest, North Carolina

ACKNOWLEDGMENTS

Because of his "trail angel" support during my Anniversary Trip and his invaluable assistance in preparing and delivering the materials for this book, I first express infinite gratitude to John Shaffer, my brother.

During those last hectic weeks in Maine, Dave Donaldson walked the Trail with me. I credit him for keeping me going.

Other memorable trail angels were Gail and Dan Johnson of South Carolina; Pat and Bob Peoples of Kincora Hostel in Hampton, Tennessee; Ed and Mary Ann Williams of Virginia; Bruce Pettingill of "Hiker's Paradise" in Gorham, New Hampshire; Henry and Carla Lafleur of Massachusetts; and Earle and Margie Towne of "The Cabin" in Andover, Maine.

My nephew Bob Shaffer provided some of my equipment and offered me words of encouragement, coming all the way from Seattle to see me off at the beginning and to greet me as I approached the end.

After we came down from Mount Katahdin, Irving "Buzz" Caverly, Superintendent of Baxter State Park, was most hospitable in providing us lodging.

To all of these people I am most grateful.

I'd also like to note that I originally intended to publish the record of my Anniversary Trip as an ode in the manner of the epic poems of hundreds of years ago. The account of my hike appears in this book in journal format, rather than that of a traditional ode, but still pays homage to the Trail, as do Bart Smith's photographs.

I dedicate this book to Benton MacKaye, whose dream came true through the unceasing efforts of Myron Avery, Jean Stephenson, and many other volunteers who have worked on the Trail to the present. They are the "trail people," so called by Adelaide Storey at a camp in Maine.

—Earl Shaffer

When I'm hiking with a backpack full of food, film, and 50 pounds of other stuff, I sometimes think of myself as a self-contained unit. But the reality is that I rely on a whole cadre of people, especially when I'm photographing along a trail so far from home.

First and foremost, I thank my wife, Bridgie, for allowing me the luxury of time. Thank goodness for the high cost of health care, because Bridgie's job as a nurse helped to facilitate this project.

Living on the West Coast, I needed a "home" on the East Coast where I could rest and store equipment. I was lucky to find three such homes where I was welcomed like a member of the family. A huge thank-you to Ralph, Helen, Sally, and Maggie Linden in McLean, Virginia; George and Phoebe Harding in Philadelphia; and John and Lois Shaffer in York, Pennsylvania. Your help was indispensable.

Thanks also to "Bill from Atlanta," Karen Berger, the Doyle Hotel, Elmer Hall of the Sunnybank Inn, Jon Hess, Maggie and Paul Kuliga at "The Barn," Laurie Potteiger, the Front Royal Motel, the Stratton Motel, "Twice," Don Wilson, and "U-Turn."

A special thanks to the kind folks at Mt. Rogers Outfitters in Damascus, Virginia, for repairing my boots, and to ITC in Lenox, Massachusetts, for repairing my tripod. Finally, a hearty thanks to all the volunteers who keep the Appalachian Trail navigable.

I dedicate this book to my mother, Ann Townsend, and to my stepson, Matt Graham.

—Bart Smith

International Standard Book Number: 1-56579-382-X

Text copyright: Earl Shaffer, 2001. All rights reserved.
Photography copyright: Bart Smith, 2001. All rights reserved.

Editor: Jenna Samelson
Design and Production: Craig Keyzer

Published by:
Westcliffe Publishers, Inc.
P.O. Box 1261
Englewood, CO 80150
www.westcliffepublishers.com

Printed in Hong Kong by: C&C Offset Printing Co., Ltd.

Library of Congress Cataloging-in-Publication Data:

Shaffer, Earl V. (Earl Victor)
  The Appalachian Trail : calling me back to the hills / text
by Earl Shaffer ; photography by Bart Smith.
    p. cm.
  ISBN 1-56579-382-X
  1. Hiking--Appalachian Trail. 2. Hiking--Appalachian Trail--Pictorial
works. 3. Shaffer, Earl V. (Earl Victor)--Journeys--Appalachian Trail.
4. Appalachian Trail--Description and travel. I. Smith, Bart, 1959- II. Title.

GV199.42.A68 S518 2001
796.51'0974--dc21
00-068572

For more information about other fine books and calendars from Westcliffe Publishers, please contact your local bookstore, call us at 1-800-523-3692, write for our free color catalog, or visit us on the Web at **www.westcliffepublishers.com.**

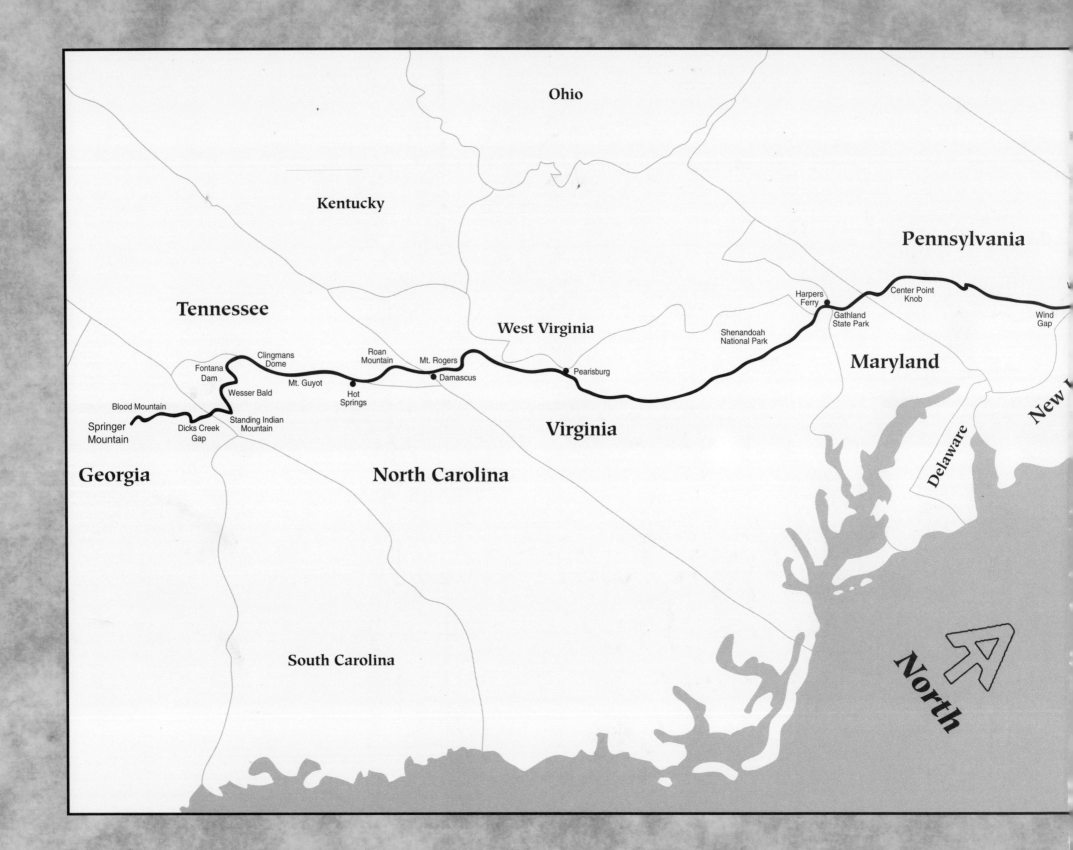